Dienberg, Eggensperger, Engel, Kohl (Hrsg./Eds.)

… am Ende ganz allein?

… eventually all alone?

Thomas Dienberg,
Thomas Eggensperger,
Ulrich Engel,
Bernhard Kohl (Hrsg./Eds.)

… am Ende ganz allein?

Gemeinschaftsbildung in post-traditionalen Zeiten

… eventually all alone?

Community-building in post-traditional times

Aschendorff
Verlag

www.aschendorff-buchverlag.de

Satz: satzbild, Philipp Czogalla

Printed in Germany
Gedruckt auf säurefreiem, alterungsbeständigem Papier ♾

ISBN: 978-3-402-13261-6
ISBN (E-Book-PDF): 978-3-402-13262-3

Inhalt // Contents

Vorwort

Jean-Luc Nancy versteht jede soziale Existenz als singulär und plural zugleich.[1] Singulär ist ein Individuum nur dann und insofern es mit und unter allen anderen ist, da Singularität paradoxerweise nicht für sich allein zu haben ist. Dieses singulär plurale Sein lässt sich nicht auf einen Pol hin entspannen, sondern trägt vielmehr eine unaufhebbare Spannung in soziale Bezüge hinein, die zwischen Einheit und Vielheit, Identität und Nicht-Identität changiert.

Als Schlüsselwort hierfür führt Nancy die Silbe *cum* ein: „Die Existenz jedoch ist *mit*: oder es existiert nichts. [...] Das Zu-Mehreren-zusammen-sein ist die ursprüngliche Situation: [...] Auf dieses ‚Ursprüngliche' oder auf dieses ‚Transzendentale' ‚geht' man nicht ‚zurück', es ist zu jeder Existenz und jedem Denken strikt gleichzeitig"[2].

Dies bedeutet, dass es eine Vielzahl sozialer Existenzen, eine Vielzahl von Welten gibt, die inkommensurabel sind. Zwischen den Sinnhorizonten dieser sozialen Existenzen und Welten besteht eine irreduzible Fremdheit, sodass der eine große Sinn, die eine kohärente Interpretation von Welt nicht (mehr) existiert. Demnach ist die Welt eine gemachte, anstatt eine gegebene. „Wir machen Sinn."[3] Dabei ist der Ursprung dieses Sinns nicht ein *Ich*, sondern ein *Wir*, da eben jede Existenz unausweichlich mit dem Faktum der Pluralität konfrontiert ist. Sinn gibt es aber wie Existenz nicht im Singular, sondern allein in der Vielheit. Der Andere sieht die Welt anders als ich, weswegen es nicht das *Wir* gibt. Für Nancy ist also wichtig, dass Vielheit der

1 J.-L. Nancy, Singulär plural sein, Zürich/Berlin 2012, 57ff.
2 Ebd., 23.71.
3 Ebd., 22.

unhintergehbare Ausgangspunkt und nicht das Ergebnis eines zufälligen Zerstreuungsprozesses einer ursprünglichen Einheit ist.[4]

Hinzu tritt eine beinahe Heisenbergsche Unschärferelation: Die beiden komplementären *Teilchen* von Gemeinschaft, das *Wir* und das *Ich*, sind nicht gleichzeitig beliebig genau bestimmbar. Wird eine Vorstellung von Gemeinschaft bzw. eines *Wir* definiert und dadurch fixiert, folgt fast automatisch ein gewaltsamer Zugriff auf das Individuum, das *Ich*, welches in eben diese Definition von Gemeinschaft gezwängt werden muss. Umgekehrt kommt es durch eine Überbestimmung des Individuums zu Schwierigkeiten bei der Findung einer wie auch immer gearteten Grundlage für ein verbindendes und gemeinschaftlich gelebtes *Wir*.

Diese faktische Gegebenheit von Vielfalt und das Changieren zwischen *Wir* und *Ich* führen dazu, dass der Zusammenhalt einer Gemeinschaft in einem nicht stillzustellenden oder abzuschließenden Prozess besteht, dass die Kohäsionskräfte einer Gemeinschaft immer wieder neu bestimmt und ausgehandelt werden müssen, wofür aber keine Metaregeln oder Metadiskurse existieren. Die Vorläufigkeit aller gemeinschaftsbildenden Prozesse impliziert Gemeinschaft als ein nie fixierbares Resultat von Diskursen oder auch Streitfällen der Interpretationen.

Zu den momentan beobachtbaren Diskursen, Prozessen und Streitfällen um Vergemeinschaftung gehören so unterschiedliche und teilweise gegenläufige Entwicklungen wie ein großes zivilgesellschaftliches Engagement für geflüchtete Menschen und die „Identitäre Bewegung“, die Suche nach nachhaltigen und fairen ökonomischen Modellen und der global-kapitalistische Markt mit seinem Streben nach individuellem Profit und Wohlstand für wenige auf Kosten vieler „Anderer“, politische Utopisten und Populisten und gesellschaftliche Inklusions- und Exklusionserfahrungen und ihre Mechanismen. Dazu gehören aber auch ganz konkrete Experimente, die gemeinsam und immer wieder neu zu buchstabieren versuchen was es bedeuten und wie es funktionieren kann in Familien, Ordensgemeinschaften, Partnerschaften, Kommunen, Initiativen usw., gemeinsam Leben zu gestalten.

4 Vgl. Th. Bedorf, Verkennende Anerkennung. Über Identität und Politik, Berlin 2010, 206.

Im Hintergrund steht dabei die Frage nach den Kohäsionskräften, die heutige Gesellschaften – und darin die kirchlichen Gemeinschaften als Teil der Zivilgesellschaft – zusammenhalten. Nicht zuletzt deswegen, weil die Frage nach diesem gesellschaftlichen Zusammenhalt unter dem Einfluss gesellschaftlicher Pluralisierungsphänomene nicht mehr einfach normativ beantwortet werden kann, bedarf es neuer Verstehens- und Interpretationsansätze.

Nach solchen Ansätzen suchte das Forschungsprojekt „Gemeinschaftsbildung in Gesellschaft, Kirche und Orden unter pluralen Bedingungen", welches von 2014 bis 2016 in einer Kooperation der Philosophisch-Theologischen Hochschule Münster (PTH) und des Institut M.-Dominique Chenu Berlin (IMDC) durchgeführt wurde. Den Abschluss des Forschungsprojekts bildete ein Symposium in Wien im September 2016, dessen Dokumentation, die das ganze Projekt noch einmal bündelt, hier nun vorliegt. Viele Personen, die das Projekt begleitet haben und denen die Projektverantwortlichen in dessen Verlauf begegnet sind, sind mit eigenen Beiträgen vertreten.

Die Frage nach dem „Ich cum Wir" oder dem „Wir cum Ich", das Changieren zwischen Individualität und Gemeinschaft, der Unabdingbarkeit beider und der positiven Rezeption von gesellschaftlicher Vielfalt trug das Forschungsprojekt durchgängig, was sich in seiner Konzeption und den Veranstaltungen zeigte. Außerdem wird dies auch in der Gestaltung des vorliegenden Sammelbandes deutlich, in dem jeweils am Projekt beteiligte Personen aus ihrer Situation heraus, d. h. aus ihrem spezifischen Länderkontext, aus ihrem fachspezifischen Blickwinkel, aus der Perspektive ihrer Lebensform etc. auf Thesenpapiere zu den Themen Gesellschaft, Kirche und Orden reagieren.

Das Projekt war interdisziplinär angelegt, was sich in verschiedenen Fachgesprächen und Veranstaltungen mit Medien- und Wirtschaftsvertreter*innen in Frankfurt und Münster und Mitarbeiter*innen des Bereichs Pastoral des Sekretariats der Deutschen Bischofskonferenz zum Thema „Neue Gemeinschaftsformen im urbanen Raum. Barcamps, Guerillagärten & Tauschläden als innovative Lern- und Lebensorte des Glaubens?" in Berlin zeigte.

Darüber hinaus war unser Projekt international konzipiert. Eine Forschungsreise führte nach Mexiko und in die USA, wo in Mexico Ciudad, Saltillo, Tijuana und San Diego u. a. Begegnungen mit

Vertreter*innen der *Universidad Iberoamericana Santa Fé*, der *Universidad Iberoamericana Tijuana*, mit Menschenrechtsaktivist*innen der Diözese Saltillo, dem Bischof von Saltillo, Raúl Vera López OP, mit Dozierenden der *Franciscan School of Theology Oceanside* und der *University of San Diego* zu unterschiedlichsten Aspekten des „Neuen Wir" möglich waren. Ein Kolloquium mit Wissenschaftler*innen fand an der *Freien Universität Amsterdam* und am *DSTS – Dominicaans Studiecentrum vor Theologie en Samenleving* zu *Multiple Religious Belonging* und zum Projekt *Een nieuw Wij* statt.

Die in das Projekt eingebundenen Akteure wiesen eine bereichernde Pluralität auf. So konnte ein Workshop mit franziskanischen und dominikanischen Ausbildungsverantwortlichen zum Thema „Gemeinschaftsbildung in Gesellschaft, Kirche und Orden unter pluralen Bedingungen" in Köln stattfinden und ein Seminar mit Dozierenden der PTH Münster zum Thema „Gemeinschaft und Individualisierung. Was hält Gesellschaft, Kirche und Orden zusammen?" in Hamburg. Aus diesem Dozierendenseminar ging der Band „Auf der Suche nach einem neuen ‚Wir'. Theologische Beiträge zu Gemeinschaft und Individualisierung" hervor, der das Seminar dokumentiert.

Wir bedanken uns bei allen, die am Zustandekommen der vorliegenden Dokumentation des Wiener Symposiums beigetragen haben. Zu nennen sind zuerst die Autor*innen der hier veröffentlichten Texte. Die meisten Beiträger*innen haben ihre Reflexionen in Wien zur Diskussion gestellt. Einige andere (Michaela Pfadenhauer, José de Jesús Legorreta Zepeda und Joseph P. Chinnici) haben wir eingeladen, die Sammlung mit ihren Reaktionen ex extra zu ergänzen.

Zu danken haben wir darüber hinaus Sharon Padilla (Bonn), die den im Original spanischen Text von José de Jesús Legorreta Zepeda ins Englische übersetzt hat und Bernd Janzen (San Diego), der die drei Thesenpapiere vom Deutschen ins Englische übertragen hat. Mareike Gerundt (IUNCTUS, Münster) schulden wir Dank für die redaktionelle Überarbeitung der Beiträge; John Solheid (Toronto) danken wir für die Korrektur des Textes von Raúl Vera López.

Last but not least sagen wir dem Aschendorff Verlag (Münster) in Person seines Lektors Dr. Bernward Kröger Danke für die gewohnt unkomplizierte und erfreulich professionelle Zusammenarbeit.

Ohne die Tagung in Wien gäbe es dieses Buch nicht. In diesem Zusammenhang gilt unser Dank Tobias Schrörs (Schwäbisch Gmünd) für seine umsichtige Organisation des Symposiums und die es begleitende Pressearbeit.

Münster und Berlin an Pfingsten 2017

Thomas Dienberg OFMCap
Thomas Eggensperger OP
Ulrich Engel OP
Bernhard Kohl OP

Preface

Jean-Luc Nancy understands each social existence as both singular and plural at once.[1] An individual is only singular if and to the extent that he or she is with and amongst everyone else, for singularity is, paradoxically, not possible in isolation. This singular plural being cannot be made one or the other; it brings a tension into social relations that cannot be relieved and that moves between uniformity and diversity, and between identity and non-identity.

Nancy introduces the syllable *cum* as the keyword here. "Existence is *with*: otherwise nothing exists. [...] Being-many-together is the originary situation; [...] there is no 'getting back to' or 'up to' this 'originary' or 'transcendental' position; the with is strictly contemporaneous with all existence, as it is with all thinking."[2]

This means that there are multiple social existences; multiple worlds, which are incommensurable. Between the horizons of meaning of these social existences and worlds is an irreducible strangeness, so that the one great meaning, the one coherent interpretation of world does not exist or no longer exists. The world is on this basis constructed rather than a given. "We make sense."[3] At the origin of this sense is not *I*, but *We*, as each existence is inevitably confronted with the fact of plurality. Yet like being, sense exists not in the singular but only in multiplicity. The 'other' sees the world differently from me, which is why the *We* does not exist. To Nancy, therefore, it is important that multiplicity is the fundamental starting point and not the result of a random process of dispersal of an original uniformity.[4]

1 J.-L. Nancy, Singulär plural sein, Zürich/Berlin 2012, 57ff. Translation taken from: http://english.columbia.edu/files/english/content/Nancy.pdf [Accessed: 04/08/2017].
2 Ibid., 23.71.
3 Ibid., 22.
4 Cf. Th. Bedorf, Verkennende Anerkennung. Über Identität und Politik, Berlin 2010, 206.

Added to this is an uncertainty principle almost worthy of Heisenberg: the more precisely we define one of the two complementary *particles* of community, the *We* and the *I*, the less precisely we can define the other. If a concept of community or of *We* is defined and therefore fixed, this almost automatically violently affects the individual, the *I*, which then has to be forced into this specific definition of community. Conversely, overdefining the individual makes it difficult to find any type of basis for a binding *We* lived out in community.

As a result of this reality of multiplicity and the movement between *We* and *I*, the cohesion of a community lies in a process that cannot be halted or completed; the cohesive powers of a community must constantly be redefined and renegotiated, but no metarules or metadiscourses exist for this task. The temporary nature of all community-building processes means that community is a result, and a result that can never be fixed, of discourses or indeed conflicts relating to interpretation.

The discourses, processes and conflicts currently surrounding the formation of community include such differing and in some cases opposing developments as a widespread commitment on the part of civil society for refugees and the "identitarian movement"; the search for fair and sustainable economic models and the global capitalist market with its quest for individual profit and prosperity for the few at the expense of many "others"; political utopians and populists and experiences of social inclusion and exclusion and their mechanisms. Yet developments also include some practical experiments, in which people, in partnership, are constantly seeking to redefine what it means to shape life together in families, religious orders, partnerships, municipalities, initiatives etc. and how that process can work.

In the background is the question of the cohesive powers that hold together today's societies – including church communities, which are part of civil society. Not least because the question of this social cohesion can no longer simply be answered in normative terms on the basis of social pluralisation phenomena, we need new approaches to understanding and interpretation.

Finding such approaches was the aim of the research project "*Gemeinschaftsbildung in Gesellschaft, Kirche und Orden unter pluralen Bedingungen*" ["Community-building in Society, the Church and

Orders in a Plural Environment"], which was conducted between 2014 and 2016 by the Philosophisch-Theologische Hochschule Münster (PTH) in cooperation with the Institut M.-Dominique Chenu Berlin (IMDC). The research project concluded with a symposium in Vienna in September 2016. The symposium papers and findings have now been published in a volume that provides a summary of the project as a whole. Many of those who were involved in and interviewed for the project have contributed.

The question of the "I with We" or the "We with I", the movement between individuality and community, the indispensability of both and the positive reception of social multiplicity defined the research project throughout, and this can be seen in its design and in the events that defined it. It is also clearly reflected in the structure of this volume, in which people involved in the project respond in the context of their circumstances, i.e. from a specific country context, from their specific perspective, from the perspective of their way of life etc. to papers on the issues of society, church and orders.

The project was interdisciplinary, and this is reflected in the range of expert discussions and events with representatives of the media and business in Frankfurt and Münster and with representatives of the Pastoral Office of the Secretariat of the German Bishops' Conference on the question of "*Neue Gemeinschaftsformen im urbanen Raum. Barcamps, Guerillagärten & Tauschläden als innovative Lern- und Lebensorte des Glaubens?*" ["New forms of community in an urban setting. BarCamps, guerrilla gardens & swap shops: innovative spaces for growing in and living out faith?"] in Berlin.

Our project was also international. There was a research trip to Mexico and the USA, where researchers were able to meet in Mexico City, Saltillo, Tijuana and San Diego with representatives of the *Universidad Iberoamericana Santa Fé* and the *Universidad Iberoamericana Tijuana*, human rights activists in the diocese of Saltillo, the Bishop of Saltillo, Raúl Vera López OP, teachers of the *Franciscan School of Theology Oceanside* and the *University of San Diego* and discuss wide-ranging aspects of the "New We". A colloquium was held with researchers at the *Freie Universität Amsterdam* and the *DSTS – Dominicaans Studiecentrum vor Theologie en Samenleving* on the subject of *Multiple Religious Belonging* and the project *Een nieuw Wij.*

Those involved in the project themselves displayed an enriching plurality: a workshop with Franciscan and Dominican tutors on *"Gemeinschaftsbildung in Gesellschaft, Kirche und Orden unter pluralen Bedingungen"* was held in Cologne and a seminar with lecturers at PTH Münster on *"Gemeinschaft und Individualisierung. Was hält Gesellschaft, Kirche und Orden zusammen?"* ["Community and individualisation. What keeps society, church and orders together?"] in Hamburg. This seminar led to the publication of *"Auf der Suche nach einem neuen ‚Wir'. Theologische Beiträge zu Gemeinschaft und Individualisierung"*, documenting the seminar.

We would like to thank all those who made this volume documenting the Vienna symposium possible. Firstly, our thanks to the authors of the texts published here. Most contributors presented their reflections for discussion in Vienna; a number of others (Michaela Pfadenhauer, José de Jesús Legorreta Zepeda and Joseph P. Chinnici) were invited by us to add their responses to complement the collection.

Our thanks also to Sharon Padilla (Bonn), who translated the original Spanish text by José de Jesús Legorreta Zepeda into English, and to Bernd Janzen (San Diego), who translated the three papers from German to English. We thank Mareike Gerundt (IUNCTUS, Münster) for editing the contributions; We thank John Solheid (Toronto) for the proofreading of the text of Raúl Vera Lopez.

Last but not least, our thanks to Aschendorff Verlag (Münster) in the person of proof-reader Dr. Bernward Kröger for his as always uncomplicated and refreshingly professional work.

This book would not have been written had it not been for the Vienna conference. Our thanks therefore also go to Tobias Schrörs (Schwäbisch Gmünd) for his excellent organisation of the symposium and the corresponding press work.

Münster and Berlin at Pentecost 2017

Thomas Dienberg OFMCap
Thomas Eggensperger OP
Ulrich Engel OP
Bernhard Kohl OP

Raúl Vera López

Let us celebrate Community

You shall love your neighbor as yourself...
Love is the fulfilling of the law
(Cf. Mt. 22.37–40; Rom. 13.9–10)

1. Current events in Mexico. As an introduction.

A few days ago, in Mexico, institutions and conservative groups got organized to protest nationally against gay people or members of the LGBTI, forcing to establish a single type of family they call of original design, which consists of mom, dad, daughter, and son. They put into question laws that censored issues of sexual education in primary education, denigrating and pointing at those with non-heterosexual preferences, and stigmatizing them. The excuse was a presidential initiative to amend the Federal Civil Code that entitled equality for marriage, to establish divorce without cause expression, to adopt and guarantee the identity of any person. That is to say, in a country that is falling apart, equal rights should not be a threat to anyone.

They are not only against the right of these people to make a family or a couple, but they indicate as valid only one model to live in community. Nowadays, life is made and shared not only between same sex people because they have found love, but also between friends, seniors who share a home, adult women and men without parents decide to live single, and perhaps have a pet for company. Single people adopt children or adults who have been abandoned maybe for heterosexuals by different circumstances, heterosexual and homosexual couples adopt to generously share life, gives study and love to one or more brethren who have no mother or father near them. And I need to mention the divorced and remarried ones, that are still looking for happiness, enlarging their familiar environment, making fraternal and social networks.

All these manifestations are against the different types of family, like us, who, leaving everything, moving away from our families, integrate ourselves to the charisms of religious families in which we want to give the best of our talents and services for the good of the communities where we can influence and make a promotion of people, so the kingdom of God can be felt in their midst, and gospel values can be reproduced with the freedom that arises from him around a total life for our sisters and brothers. When a monk makes a vow, he does it for the kingdom of heaven, on the understanding that it exists when the whole human family is living what God wants for his children without exception. That is, we leave everything to build the great family, experimenting and expanding the family warmth and love in the middle of the ecclesial community, but mainly in the human community.

In these families like in all, the differences, asymmetries and the diverse profiles, increase the wealth of the family, especially if it walks like Jesus, with the otherness, and more if that other person is poor, ill, excluded, untouchable or distant and we went to speak of love, forgiveness, acceptance and celebration. We can hate Starbucks, its prices, wages, the displacement of local cafeterias, but they do make family in a kindest way –sometimes– better than we do, talking to each of its children by its name and knowing them. There are many places with people who want to hear their names and wait until the good news arrives. The contemplation of the face of God must take us to contemplate the face of other brothers and sisters. It is necessary to go together in this search; with them we will get a sense for our consecrated life.

2. The God of life in us.

God is definitely on the side of life, as the book of Wisdom says: "Because God did not make death, nor does he rejoice in the destruction of the living. For he fashioned all things that they might have being; and the creatures of the world are wholesome. And there is not a destructive drug among them nor any domain of the nether world on earth" (Wis. 1.13–14).

In the book of Deuteronomy, the concern of God for the care of the life of each and every one of his children of his people is very sharp. He warns the Israelites very strongly that, above all else, He will take care of the most vulnerable people, including the poor. In the prophetic language, these people will have a more specific identification: exploited workers, widows, orphans, and strangers. The text refers firstly that, given the abundance of blessings that the people have received, there is no justification for poverty: "Since the Lord, your God, will bless you abundantly in the land he will give you to occupy as your heritage, there should be no one of you in need", (Deut. 15:4).

The following warning is that if there is any poor in any of the cities of Israel, they cannot gloss over the situation, but should move themselves to take that person out of that status, they cannot ignore it: "If one of your kinsmen in any community is in need in the land which the Lord, your God, is giving you, you shall not harden your heart nor close your hand to him in his need. Instead, you shall open your hand to him and freely lend him enough to meet his need" (Deut. 15.7–8). This is the stance of Pope Francis, we cannot turn human beings into waste matter, because this is a very clear sign of a dehumanized society. He points out very clearly the structural mistakes made in the contemporary world, as they systematically generate the exclusion of millions of people.

The third warning means that we must remain watchful, looking at the signs of the times as Jesus warns in the Gospel (Cf. Lk. 12.54–59), to warn ourselves and those around us, about the situation regarding human rights in our society. For, if we get accustomed to living among the homeless, battered women, victims of enforced disappearance, children dying prematurely, youth without a future, etc., and we do nothing to change this situation, then we are not showing ourselves as followers of Jesus, neither are we his children, nor do we have faith in the God for whom we live. The God who presents us the Lord Jesus is in favor of life irrevocably and decisively. That is why the text of Deuteronomy warned the Israelites: "The needy will never be lacking in the land; that is why I command you to open your hand to your poor and needy kinsman in your country" *(Deut. 15:4.7–8.11).*

The prophet Elijah is the man *par excellence* who learned first-hand that God is the Lord of life. He knew it with certainty during the three years with drought in the Samaria region. Because he remained alive, obeying the command of God who sent him to live on the banks of Qerit river, from which he drank water. And he was provided food by ravens, by which God preserved his life sending him bread and meat. When the stream of the river was exhausted, by God's command Elijah went to live in Sarepta. There, God kept the prophet's life, as well as the life of a widow with whom he had lodging, and her son, through the promise made to the widow by the word of Elijah, that she would not be missing the flour in the jar, or oil in her house, while the drought remained in that region. After a while, while Elijah was still a guest in that home, the son of the widow died. Elijah was sure that God kenosis wanted the child's life, and asked for his intervention to resurrect him, so it was. The prophet returned him alive to his mother, and she knew and was convinced that Elijah was truly a man of God, and that he had the word of God who gives life. (Cf. 1 Kgs. 17.4–24).

God is also in favor of life, through the prophet Jeremiah, whom he orders to spread his word to the king as follows: "You shall say: Listen to the word of the Lord, king of Judah, who sit on the throne of David, you, your ministers, and your people that enter by these gates! Thus says the Lord: Do what is right and just. Rescue the victim from the hand of his oppressor. Do not wrong or oppress the resident alien, the orphan, or the widow, and do not shed innocent blood in this place. Woe to him who builds his house on wrong, his terraces on injustice; who works his neighbor without pay, and gives him no wages. Who says, "I will build myself a spacious house, with airy rooms", who cuts out windows for it, panels it with cedar, and paints it with vermillion. Must you prove your rank among kings by competing with them in cedar? Did not your father eat and drink? He did what was right and just, and it went well with him. Because he dispensed justice to the weak and the poor, it went well with him. Is this not true knowledge of me? says the Lord. But your eyes and heart are set on nothing except on your own gain, on shedding innocent blood, on practicing oppression and extortion" (Jer. 22:2–3.13–17).

Likewise, God is manifested decidedly on behalf of life when, through the prophet Isaiah, He speaks of the conditions in which the people come to present their offerings in the temple of

Jerusalem: "When you come in to visit me, who asks these things of you? Trample my courts no more! Bring no more worthless offerings; your incense is loathsome to me. New moon and Sabbath, calling of assemblies, octaves with wickedness: these I cannot bear. Your new moons and festivals I detest; they weigh me down, I tire of the load. When you spread out your hands, I close my eyes to you; Though you pray the more, I will not listen. Your hands are full of blood! Wash yourselves clean! Put away your misdeeds from before my eyes; cease doing evil; learn to do good. Make justice your aim: redress the wronged, hear the orphan's plea, defend the widow" (Isa. 1.12–17).

Jesus himself told his disciples that, when any of them were to make an offering to God, if facing Him he remembers that a brother had a complaint against him, he should leave his gift at the altar, and go to be reconciled with his brother, then his offering would accepted by God (Cf. Mt. 5.23–24). The Gospel of Saint Luke, meanwhile, quotes the words with which Jesus asks those who analyze the signs of weather issues, because they know how to distinguish among those announcing that there will be rain or heat, so he asks them why they couldn't distinguish what happens around them, or between what is truly fair, and what is not. (Cf. Lk. 12.54–56). Both Matthew and Luke, after the texts just cited, about suspending the offering if there is something to be solved and when they talk about the need to analyze the context that surrounds us in accordance with justice and what is not fair, Jesus gives us the following recommendation for both situations: "If you are to go with your opponent before a magistrate, make an effort to settle the matter on the way; otherwise your opponent will turn you over to the judge, and the judge hand you over to the constable, and the constable throw you into prison. I say to you, you will not be released until you have paid the last penny" (Cf. Lk. 12.58–59; Mt. 5.25–26).

In the context of Luke's Gospel, this warning must be understood in light of the texts of the book of Deuteronomy to which I referred above, because a good part of Chapter 12, at the end of which comes this warning of Jesus. He has referred to the fair administration of the goods of the earth, that God has placed for the benefit of all and not just for a few (Cf. Lk. 12.13–46). Jesus, in the same line of the prophets, is in favor of full life for all women and men who inhabit this planet (Cf. Jn. 10:10). We can understand that along our passage through this world, we must always bear in mind that this adversary, who can put us before the judge where we can get out losing, represents the poor from any part of the earth, as the worker of the parable (Lk. 12.13–21) who had a bumper harvest and believed that all that meant that he could lead a free life for himself for the rest of his days. He was wrong, because that night God would ask for his soul, so, what would it profit him to keep those goods? The lapidary sentence of Jesus at the end of the parable is: "Thus will it be for the one who stores up treasure for himself but is not rich in what matters to God" (Lk. 12:21). Therefore, the life that those assets would produce was especially for the life of the poorest who were around him, and also for those that remained in poverty because of the selfish dynamics of men like that peasant introduced into society. God is for the life of everyone, not just a few privileged people. The mistake of the ranchman is the same as the one made by the rich man to the poor Lazarus, since he did not care for the life of his brother (Lk. 16.19–31).

In the parable of the Good Samaritan (Lk. 10.29–37) Jesus gives us a profound lesson to always stay close to those most in need and their lives. In contrast to the priest and the Levite, who took a detour so not to pass by the man beaten and robbed by thieves that left him half dead, the Samaritan cares about the risk to his life, and he comes over to him, heals immediately his wounds with oil and wine that he has with him, and puts him up into his horse and takes him to a hostelry. He delays his trip one day to serve him, leaves some money to be attended by the host, and he offers to pay at his return whatever it takes until he is fully recovered. This parable, like the Prodigal Son (Lk. 15.11–32), is a wonderful teaching that in the sight of God, there are no limits for us, his children, to have life and to have it in abundance. This is indicated in the words that the merciful father offers to the son who had left home and had wasted the money from his father: "Quickly bring the finest robe and put it on him; put a ring on his finger and sandals on his feet. Take the fattened calf and slaughter it. Then let us celebrate with a feast, because this son of mine was dead, and has come to life again; he was lost, and has been found" (Lk.15.22–24). In both parables, we can identify perfectly God's attitude toward us. In both the Good Samaritan and in the father of the Prodigal Son, Jesus draws us to his Heavenly Father and Himself, because: "The Son cannot do anything on his own, but only what he sees the Father doing; for what He does, the Son will do also" (Jn. 5:19).

We are servants of God, who is a Father full of mercy and infinite love for his child, who does not stop looking for wherever is located and under the conditions his son is. He will always seek, and will always wait. This is the meaning of our consecration to Him in our religious profession. We unite mind and heart to the realization of his project: The unity of the whole human family, of all his daughters and sons of God scattered by sin (Cf. Jn. 11.49–53). We're joined intensely to the mystery of his death and resurrection, that is the redemptive power of the Passover of Jesus: "I have come to set the earth on fire, and how I wish it were already blazing! There is a baptism with which I must be baptized, and how great is my anguish until it is accomplished!" (Lk. 12.49–50). "All power in heaven and on earth has been given to me. Go, therefore, and make disciples of all nations, baptizing them in the name of the Father, and of the Son, and of the holy Spirit, teaching them to observe all that I have commanded you. And behold, I am with you always, until the end of the age" (Mt. 28.18–20).

3. Positioning of the individual as part of the world. Overview of the Holy Father.

If our body is made up of land, air, water; if the earth is our common home, our mother earth and our sister; if the land is battered and pillaged; what should we do with our existence and our time on this earth. The Encyclical Letter Laudato Si' (2015) presents the phenomenon of Ecology holistically and begins to relate in a precise manner the environment with economic and social issues.

Holy Father Francis focuses his gaze upon the world from the concept of God's Kingdom, the project that Jesus established by overcoming the domain of the evil spirit over the world through his death and resurrection. There are great words of Jesus in this regard, as they approached the days of his passion, which are conveyed in the Gospel of John: "Now is the time of judgment on this world; now the ruler of this world will be driven out. And when I am lifted up from the earth, I will draw everyone to myself" (Jn. 12.31–32).

This theological approach to understanding the reign of God over the world, which began with the death and glorification of Jesus Christ through his resurrection and ascension into heaven, to reign over the universe, leads the Pope to give us a wide view of the phenomena occurring in the world today, and to confront them with more open approaches that break with the narrow doctrinal systems that have emerged in some parts of the Church, from a comprehension of it far from the concept of the People of God, to which we are called to belong as members of the human family. The teachings of the Church since the Second Vatican Council have left behind a reduced vision of the Church, understood as a religious system justified by a closed doctrinal system, which only certain kinds of people can, and whom the same system considered *ad hoc* people to enter into their ranks, and are therefore eligible to be part of the perfect society that -they believe- must be the Church.

From a vision of the Church as a community of disciples of Jesus, Pope Francis enlightens current problems regarding the word of God, with criteria that are open to seek solutions, and that integrate especially those most abandoned and excluded, for whom God also puts at their service all the resources and the magnificence of his creation. The Holy Father has clearly and decisively undertaken a prophetic complaint against the way the powerful of the earth, in the financial, economic and political order, have perversely put under their service all the advantages science and technology provide to the human being, to manage all the planet's resources without imposing an ethical perspective, to market without any control, and develop a frenetic industrial, financial and commercial activity, which is targeting only a selfish gain and profit at any human cost.

When peasants, members of indigenous communities, and those living in marginalized areas of urban spaces, are hindrances for businessmen and public servers trying to occupy territories and enjoy the resources that they are interested to sell or use for their own purposes, they will dismiss the citizens with elements of the police, army and paramilitary groups to evict them, imprisoning them or eliminating them. For those who only have money and power, the cost of human life is less than minerals, resources and uses of our mother earth, and our brothers.

In Laudato Si' we find a reflection about the environment and the relationship between nature and the society living in it. "Nature cannot be regarded as something separate from ourselves or as a mere setting in which we live. We are part of nature, included in it and thus in constant interaction with it. Recognizing the reasons why a given area is polluted requires a study of the workings of society, its economy, its behavior patterns, and the ways it grasps reality. Given the scale of change, it is no longer possible to find a specific, discrete answer for each part of the problem. It is essential to seek comprehensive solutions which consider the interactions within natural systems themselves and with social systems. We are faced not with two separate crises, one environmental and the other social, but rather with one complex crisis which is both social and environmental. Strategies for a solution demand an integrated approach to combating poverty, restoring dignity to the excluded, and at the same time protecting nature" (n. 139).

> *Economic growth tends to produce predictable reactions and a certain standardization with the aim of simplifying procedures and reducing costs. This suggests the need for an 'economic ecology' capable of appealing to a broader vision of reality. The protection of the environment is in fact 'an integral part of the development process and cannot be considered in isolation from it'. We urgently need a humanism capable of bringing together the different fields of knowledge, including economics, in the service of a more integral and integrating vision. Today, the analysis of environmental problems cannot be separated from the analysis of human, family, work-related and urban contexts, nor from how individuals relate to themselves (n. 141).*

> *If everything is related, then the health of a society's institutions has consequences for the environment and the quality of human life. "Every violation of solidarity and civic friendship harms the environment." In this sense, social ecology is necessarily institutional, and gradually extends to the whole of society, from the primary social group, the family, to the wider local, national and international communities. Within each social stratum, and between them, institutions develop*

> *to regulate human relationships. Anything which weakens those institutions has negative consequences, such as injustice, violence and loss of freedom... Moreover, what takes place in any one area can have a direct or indirect influence on other areas (n. 142).*

None of us can be excluded from the problems of today's world, keeping our pastoral work based on simplistic analyzes to justify our comfortable life, without deep insights, responding every day to what fits our selfish thinking.

4. Social commitment in consecrated life. Vatican II and Latin America.

The Pastoral Constitution of the Second Vatican Council (1965) "Gaudium et spes", offers us the idea of looking back to the world and its problems. The document was not applied immediately in spite of its importance not only within the church, but also in the real world, the ecumenical one, the one of so many women and men of the international community with whom we can work to have a better world for everyone, and in which we are all brothers. Speaking of the imbalances of the world, this unique Pastoral Constitution of Vatican II recognizes the human being as part of it, and therefore it also ranks her/him as one who should be part of its reconstruction: "Mutual distrust, enmities, conflicts and hardships. Of such is man at once the cause and the victim" (n. 8).

The text remains current with the most fundamental questions of our task: "What is man? What is this sense of sorrow, of evil, of death, which continues to exist despite so much progress? What purpose have these victories purchased at so high a cost? What can man offer to society, what can he expect from it? What follows this earthly life?" (n. 10). "For by his innermost nature man is a social being, and unless he relates himself to others he can neither live nor develop his potential" (n. 12).

To talk about the mission of the Church and its relationship with the contemporary world, it affirms: "Christ, to be sure, gave His Church no proper mission in the political, economic or social order. The purpose which He set before her is a religious one.

But out of this religious mission itself come a function, a light and an energy which can serve to structure and consolidate the human community according to the divine law. As a matter of fact, when circumstances of time and place produce the need, she can and indeed should initiate activities on behalf of all men, especially those designed for the needy, such as the works of mercy and similar undertakings" (n. 42).

The Episcopate of Latin America and the Caribbean has wanted to walk in a renewed way in its evangelization to the service of the communities, recognizing that Latin American peoples have the right to a fullness of life, human conditions free from hunger and from all forms of violence. In the last General Conference in Aparecida (2007), it continues its concern to ensure that the person is standing up regarding dignity, respect and justice, and to give continuity to the challenges posed especially since the ecumenical council, Vatican II (Medellin, 1968 , Puebla, 1979, Santo Domingo, 1992), where the Church participates „of the joys and hopes, the sorrows and happiness of his sons, and wants to walk beside them in this period of challenges, to always inspire hope and comfort on them" (cf. Gaudium et Spes, n. 1).

The motto of this last meeting of the Conference of Latin American Bishops was: "Disciples and missionaries of Jesus Christ, so that peoples may have life in him", in whose final document the essential task of evangelization is spoken to us: discipleship and the mission we have, including the preferential option for the poor, their promotion and their liberation, and says: "When awareness of belonging to Christ grows by reason of the gratitude and joy that it produces, the eagerness to communicate the gift of this encounter to all also grows. The mission is not limited to a program or project, but it is sharing the experience of the event of the encounter with Christ, witnessing it and announcing it from person to person, from community to community, and from the Church to the ends of the earth" (n. 145).

"In sharing this mission, the disciples journey toward holiness. Living it in mission leads them into the heart of the world. Hence, holiness is not a flight toward self-absorption or toward religious individualism, nor does it mean abandoning the urgent reality of the enormous economic, social, and political problems of Latin America and the world, let alone a flight from reality toward an exclusively spiritual world" (n. 148). "The diversity of charisms, ministries, and services opens the horizon to the everyday exercise of communion, through which the gifts of the Spirit are made available to others so that charity may abound (cf. 1 Cor 12:4–12). Each baptized person in effect bears gifts that he or she must develop in unity and complementarity with those of others so as to form the one Body of Christ, given up for the life of the world. Practical recognition of the organic unity and diversity of functions will assure greater missionary vitality and will be a sign and instrument of reconciliation and peace for our peoples. Each community is called to discover and integrate the silent hidden talents that the Spirit bestows as a gift on the faithful" (n. 162). In the people of God, "Communion and mission are profoundly connected with each other, they interpenetrate and mutually imply each other … Communion gives rise to mission and mission is accomplished in communion" (n. 163).

> *Today in Latin America and the Caribbean, consecrated life is called to be a discipleship life, fervent about Jesus-Way to the merciful Father, and hence deeply mystical and communitarian in nature. It is called to be a missionary life, fervent about proclaiming Jesus- Word of the Father; and hence radically prophetic, capable of illuminating in the light of Christ the shadows of the contemporary world and the paths of new life, and hence what is required is a prophetic witness that yearns even to surrender one's life in continuity with the tradition of holiness and martyrdom of so many religious men and women over the history of the continent. It must likewise be at the service of the world, fervent for Jesus–Life of the Father, who becomes present in the littlest ones and those who are least whom it wishes to serve from its own charism and spirituality (n. 220).*

In our Latin American reality, the suffering faces that hurt us, and for whom we have bet on a pastoral job defending their human rights, could be grouped among the following, although there will be some in other delicate situations: People living in the street in the great large cities, migrant workers, ill people, relatives of forced disappeared, land workers fighting for lands free of toxins, codependents and addicts, detainees in prisons, abused and exploited women, LGBTI members, children, adolescents, elderly, and so many people who suffer from our exclusion.

5. Being and doing family, to others and with others.

Perhaps we idealize the community in which we want to live, but if that ideal we wish for is a house, a meeting place as they promised us in our first formation communities, or if we think of it as a place of welcome and freedom, a space for prayers and common celebrations, a place where God's world is, where you can discern the cultural, social, political, economic, or personal situations, from an apostolic vision, if we want a place in this way, it means we are in the reality, wishing to transform it –for us and for others. Living incongruences, inequalities, differences of interests, by age, schedules, work or services, is to be in the midst of the reality that is lived in the world. And in the reality of society, we cannot ignore, it is necessary to work to build the kingdom of God from this earth, denouncing the unfair differences and looking for equalities, fairness and justice in a personal way, within the community, and in a regional and global way. Frustration must motivate us to work in the pursuit of the Lord Jesus Christ with greater coherence, strength and creativity. Let us not be the eldest son of the parable in the community, but the one who forgives, shows us how to celebrate, do community and cheer us for what is around us.

* * *

Zusammenfassung zu: Raúl Vera López, Lasst uns Gemeinschaft feiern!

Bischof Raúl Vera López (Saltillo | Mexiko) geht in seinem Beitrag von gegenwärtigen Entwicklungen in der mexikanischen Politik und Gesellschaft aus, die dadurch geprägt sind, dass heteronormative, diskriminierende Lebensformen politisch in der Gesellschaft durchgesetzt und zum exklusiven Maßstab menschlicher Gemeinschaft erhoben werden sollen.

Vor dem Hintergrund des II. Vatikanischen Konzils und der Enzyklika *Laudato Si'* sieht er in christlichen Gemeinschaften einen wirksamen Gegenentwurf hierzu, insbesondere dann, wenn sie sich durch die Verschiedenartigkeit und *Asymmetrien* ihrer Mitglieder, durch die Andersheit von armen Menschen und letztendlich durch die Andersheit des Vorbildes Jesu prägen lassen, was sich konkret im Einsatz für die verwundbarsten Mitglieder innerhalb einer Gesellschaft zeigt.

Dieser Einsatz ist für Raúl Vera sowohl prophetisch als auch utopisch, da er immer eine befreite Gesellschaft, d. h. eine Gesellschaft ohne Ungerechtigkeiten und Armut antizipiert. Die Rolle der Kirche besteht in diesem Zusammenhang darin, endlich ihre starre Systematik als *societas perfecta* zugunsten eines dynamischen Selbstverständnisses als Gemeinschaft der Nachfolger*innen Jesu aufzugeben und so zu einer Menschlichkeit zu gelangen, die ihr Wissen und ihre Kraft für eine *soziale und ökonomische Ökologie*, d. h. für eine integrierende Vision der Menschheit untereinander und mit ihrer Umwelt zusammenbringt.

Thomas Eggensperger / Bernhard Kohl

Thesenpapier: Gesellschaft

1. Situation

Aktuell sind in Europa gegenläufige Entwicklungen zu beobachten:

1.1 Traditionelle Vergemeinschaftungsformen schwinden.

Traditionelle Vergemeinschaftungsformen in Gesellschaft (z. B. Ehe und Familie auf der Mikroebene; die Europäische Union auf der Makroebene), Kirche (z. B. Pfarreien) ändern sich, werden schwächer und/oder zerbrechen gänzlich. Das betrifft auch die Orden.

Michael Hardt und Antonio Negri verwenden für diese Entwicklungen den Begriff des „Anthropologischen Exodus“[1]. Damit bezeichnen sie neue Lebensformen, die, wie sie schreiben, „vollkommen unfähig [sind], sich an familiäres Leben anzupassen, an Fabrikdisziplin, an die Regulierung des traditionellen Sexuallebens usw.“ Selbst wenn diese Formulierung die Sache ein wenig überzeichnet, liefern sie doch einen Ausdruck, unter dem sich eine ganze Reihe gegenwärtiger Erscheinungen rubrizieren lässt. Mit dem Begriff „Exodus“ wird ein Ab- oder Auszug bezeichnet, welcher intentional vollzogen wird und der Auswirkungen sowohl für die Ab- oder Ausziehenden als auch für eine Gesellschaft hat, aus denen sie ab- oder ausziehen. Damit müssen nicht unbedingt räumliche Wanderungen gemeint sein – wie sie natürlich in Anbetracht der Zahlen von geflüchteten Menschen eine Rolle spielen und spielen werden – sondern

1 Vgl. M. Hardt / A. Negri, Empire. Die neue Weltordnung, Frankfurt/M. / New York 2002, 227.

es kann sich auch um metaphorisch verstandene Bewegungen des „Exodus nach innen" handeln.[2]

Beispiele für solche übertragenen und engagierten Auszüge sind, sofern sie eine gewisse existenzielle Dimension umfassen, vielfach in posttraditionalen Vergemeinschaftungsformen zu finden.

1.2 Posttraditionale Vergemeinschaftungsformen nehmen zu

Zugleich sind neue, posttraditionale Formen von Gemeinschaftsbildung zu beobachten, wozu Stadtkommunen, selbstverwaltete Schulen, Kinderläden, besetzte Häuser, subsistenzorientierte Landwirtschaftsprojekte, autonom organisierte Subökonomien wie Tauschringe und Leihläden, Urban Gardening, Experimente mit Polysexualität und Polyamorie, Aneignung und Umdeutung urbaner Räume vom Guerilla Gardening und Guerilla Stricken bis hin zum Leben auf besetzten Plätzen, nicht zuletzt religiös motivierte Experimente.

Dabei sind diese Praktiken nicht einfach wüste Ausdrucksformen von Protest, sondern sie haben massive theoretische Hintergründe: Von einer Theorie der direkten Demokratie über das mutualistische Ideal der gegenseitigen Hilfe und ökologische Nachhaltigkeit bis hin zu Modellen solidarischer Ökonomie.

Diese Zunahme posttraditionaler Vergemeinschaftungsformen ist dabei nicht auf einzelne Städte oder Länder begrenzt, sondern umfasst recht allgemein zumindest die Metropolen der westlichen Staaten. Beachtenswert ist außerdem, dass die Experimente mit posttraditionalen Vergemeinschaftungsformen nicht mehr von Großorganisationen (Parteien, Gewerkschaften, Kirchen) initiiert werden, sondern sich spontan und *von unten*, auf begrenzte Zeit und in ganz persönlicher Verantwortung bilden. Sie weisen darüber hinaus oft eine bewusst spirituelle Orientierung auf.

2 Vgl. D. Loick, Stichwort: Exodus. Leben jenseits von Staat und Konsum?, in: WestEnd 1 (2014), 61–66, hier 61.

2. Implikationen

Die Veränderungen der Vergemeinschaftungsformen weisen einige interessante Implikationen auf:[3]

- Sie insistieren darauf, dass auch innerhalb kapitalistischer Gesellschaften die Etablierung nicht- oder post-kapitalistischer Freiräume oder Heterotopien möglich ist.
- Daraus folgt utopietheoretisch die Ablehnung negatorischer Kritikstrategien, welche das Ausmalen alternativer Gesellschaftsformen mit einer Art Bilderverbot belegen. Vielmehr sollen alternative Formen des Zusammenlebens sofort diskutiert, ausprobiert und revidiert werden können, ohne dass man dafür auf einen großen gesellschaftlichen Bruch warten müsste.
- Neue Vergemeinschaftungsformen sind theoretisch nicht blind, sondern übernehmen eine sowohl moralische als auch institutionentheoretische Begründungslast: Sie wollen zeigen, dass alternative Lebensformen auch diesseits einer radikalen sozialen Transformation reale Veränderungsmöglichkeiten darstellen, dass sie stabil sind und funktionieren.
- Ethisch erneuern sie den aristotelisch anmutenden Versuch, das moralisch Richtige mit der Erfahrung von Glückseligkeit zu verknüpfen. Sie legen allerdings kein Bild der Askese zugrunde, sondern versuchen einen auch für den Einzelnen attraktiven Lebensentwurf bereitzustellen.
- Weil eine posttraditionale Vergemeinschaftungsform weder die Inbesitznahme des Staates noch die argumentative Gewinnung der Mehrheit der Bevölkerung voraussetzt, kann sie graduelle Positionierungen, ein *Sowohl-als-Auch* zulassen, oder nur eine binäre Entscheidung, ein *Entweder-Oder* zu fordern.

3 Vgl. ebd., 61–63.

3. Komplikationen

Bedenken gegen die posttraditionalen Vergemeinschaftungsformen werden formuliert, indem man sie etwa als resignativ-eskapistische Strategie oder als fragwürdiges Resultat eines Begehrens nach Individualismus oder Authentizität versteht. Zu diesen Bedenken gehören:[4]

- Eine klassische Kritik an posttraditionalen Vergemeinschaftungsformen lautet, dass sie die Integrationsfähigkeit bestehender Vergemeinschaftungsformen unterschätzen und so bestenfalls wirkungslos, schlechtestenfalls ideologisch erscheinen, weil sie von der Notwendigkeit einer universellen gesellschaftlichen Veränderung, oder von der Notwendigkeit eines gesamtgesellschaftlichen Konsenses ablenken.
- Ein wichtiges demokratietheoretisches Problem und auch eine gewisse depolitisierende Tendenz besteht darin, dass posttraditionale Vergemeinschaftungsformen keine Auseinandersetzung mit Gesellschaft, Staat und Institutionen suchen – deren Kinder sie sind – und somit auf Teilhabe an der öffentlichen Diskussion verzichten.
- Schließlich scheinen derartige Praktiken regelmäßig an der Überinvestition in persönliche Beziehungen zu implodieren. Symptome einer solchen Erosion sind häufig die Überstrapazierung intimer Beziehungen, Überforderung und emotionale Überlastung, Personalisierung und Moralisierung von Konflikten.

Was bedeutet aber nun eine solche Pluralisierung von Lebens- und Beziehungsformen, was bedeuten alternative Formen der Ökonomie oder ein teilweiser Ausstieg aus Ordnung und Organisation von Gesellschaft für den Zusammenhalt von Menschen innerhalb einer solchen Gesellschaft?

4 Vgl. ebd., 63f.

4. Perspektiven

Es sind drei gesellschaftliche Großtrends zu beobachten, die es zu bewerten gilt:

4.1 Individualisierung

Der Prozess der Individualisierung betont die Autonomie des/der Einzelnen. Mit der Entwicklung selbstbestimmter Lebensformen eröffnet sich eine Fülle neuer *Optionen*. Diese stehen in Konkurrenz zu den *Ligaturen*, die traditionell und institutionell den gesellschaftlichen Zusammenhalt garantierten. Wo diese Kohäsionskräfte fehlen, erstarken Exklusionsmechanismen (z. B. nationale/nationalistische Abschottung gegen Flüchtende, gegen *den Islam*, Privatisierung des Ordenslebens, Distanz im kirchlichen Leben).[5]

Für Religion und Kirche hat diese Entwicklung Konsequenzen: Religion und Religiosität verschwinden nicht, sondern geraten in den Raum des Privaten und werden damit zunehmend unsichtbar. Religion wird zur Privatsache.[6]

Zugleich wird der Islam in Westeuropa sichtbarer (repräsentativer Moscheebau, mehr Kopftuch tragende Frauen etc.) und von Vielen als identitätsbedrohende und gewalttätige Kraft wahrgenommen, mit der man nicht recht umzugehen weiß, was Populisten wiederum auszunutzen wissen.

5 Vgl. Th. Eggensperger, Individualisierung in der Moderne. Alternativentwurf zu einem Verständnis von Säkularisierung als Folge der Modernisierung, in: Th. Dienberg / Th. Eggensperger / U. Engel (Hrsg.), Säkulare Frömmigkeit. Theologische Beiträge zu Säkularisierung und Individualisierung, Münster 2013, 105–117.

6 Vgl. J. Casanova, Europäische Säkularisierung auf globaler vergleichender Perspektive. Diagnose und Antwort, in: Th. Dienberg / Th. Eggensperger / U. Engel (Hrsg./Eds.), Himmelwärts und weltgewandt. Kirche und Orden in (post-)säkularer Gesellschaft / Heavenward and worldly. Church and Religious Orders in (Post) Secular Society, Münster 2014, 41–54.

4.2 Pluralisierung

In den spätmodernen Gesellschaften Europas sind rasante Pluralisierungstendenzen zu beobachten. Dies betrifft v.a. Lebensformen und -stile: Nichteheliche Lebensgemeinschaften, Alleinerziehende, gewählte Singleexistenzen, gleichgeschlechtliche Lebenspartnerschaften oder Ehen, Fernbeziehungen und gewollt kinderlose Ehen. Hinzu kommt eine nicht zuletzt durch Migration bedingte neue kulturelle und religiöse Vielfalt im Zusammenleben. Dauerhaft eindeutige Identitätszuschreibungen (z.B. Inländer oder Ausländer bei Menschen mit Migrationshintergrund in der 2. oder 3. Generation) stehen in Frage oder lösen sich auf. Entscheidungen zu treffen fällt vielen Menschen aufgrund der angebotenen Vielfalt zunehmend schwerer.

Der Großtrend Pluralisierung macht auch vor dem Bereich der Religion nicht halt. In der Konsequenz bilden sich auch für den Einzelnen neue Zugehörigkeitsmodelle aus, so u.a. das „Multiple Religious Belonging" (d.i. gleichzeitige Zugehörigkeit zu verschiedenen, inhaltlich miteinander konkurrierenden Religionen und Konfessionen).[7]

Es ist sinnvoll, noch differenzierter nicht nur von einer multiplen religiösen Zughörigkeit zu sprechen, sondern von einem „Multiple Social Belonging", da sich die Zugehörigkeitsvielfalt nicht nur auf im eigentlichen Sinne religiöse Bezüge reduziert. Religion, Weltanschauung und gruppenbezogene Affinitäten gehören oftmals zusammen.

Außerdem ist zu Beginn des 21. Jahrhundert ein Wunsch nach neuen Formen von Gemeinschaft festzustellen. Diesem Begehren fehlt allerdings oft die Erfahrung (z.B. in Ein-Kind-Familien) und es ist in der Vorstellung stark individualisiert. Somit ist Gemeinschaft heute keine quasi ontologische Größe mehr, die der persönlichen Absicherung dient, sondern sie muss immer neu und mühsam sozial erarbeitet werden.[8]

7 Vgl. M. Kalsky, Flexibel geloven. Zingeving voorbij de grenzen van religies, Vught 2014.

8 Vgl. B. Kohl, Die Anerkennung des Verletzbaren. Eine Rekonstruktion der negativen Hermeneutik der Gottebenbildlichkeit über die Anerkennungstheorien

4.3 Das Mundane

Es wird immer weniger plausibel, im Geflecht menschlicher Beziehungen und Anschauungen strikt zwischen dem Politischen, dem Religiösen oder dem Säkularen zu trennen. Vielmehr hat sich das Phänomen der Sichtbarkeit dieser Zuschreibungen verändert, da sie zum Teil zwar im Privaten aufgehen, aber dadurch, dass sie im Öffentlichen nicht mehr wahrnehmbar sind, dennoch weiterhin fortbestehen. Auch hier wird es das Einfachste sein, sich zur Umschreibung dessen, was Sphäre, d.h. der Raum, indem diese Attribute sich zueinander ordnen, neu zu begreifen. Eine Formulierung wie die des Postsäkularen greift dabei zu kurz, weil sie nicht auf Neues verweist, sondern auf etwas dem Bestehenden Nachfolgenden. Dies unterschätzt das Neue an der Gestaltung der anthropologischen und sozialen Verflechtung des Raumes, der nicht einfach in den privaten oder öffentlichen zu trennen ist. Wir schlagen alternativ vor, von einer „Sphäre des Mundanen" auszugehen. Das *Mundane* („mundus" = Welt) geht durchaus kongruent mit dem Politischen oder dem Öffentlichen, und auch mit dem Säkularen, ohne aber besetzt zu sein von Trennungen und Einschränkungen, die der Situation des Menschen nicht gerecht wird. Einer Sphäre des Mundanen eignet dieses *Zwischen*, in dem Menschen sich interpersonal und sozial koordinieren, gleich welcher religiösen oder weltanschaulichen Grundeinstellung sie verhaftet sind – zumal im Sinne der multiplen religiösen oder sozialen Zugehörigkeit eindeutige Zuschreibungen gar nicht mehr möglich sind.[9]

5. Sozialethische Erwägungen

Die dargestellten neuen Vergemeinschaftungsformen bilden sich u.a. gerade deswegen, um wieder menschliche Gemeinschaft zu (er) leben, die von mehr als einer Ökonomie zusammengehalten wird.

Axel Honneths und Judith Butlers und über die Theologie Edward Schillebeeckx', Würzburg 2017 (im Druck).

9 Vgl. Th. Eggensperger, Individualisierung und die Sphäre des Mundanen, in: Th. Dienberg / Th. Eggensperger / U. Engel (Hrsg./Eds.), Himmelwärts und weltgewandt / Heavenward and Worldly, a.a.O., 247–254.

Arbeitnehmer ersuchen zunehmend um angemessene Formen der gesicherten Freizeitgestaltung („Work-Life-Balance",“Sabbatical", „New Work") neben ihrer Arbeit, da es ihnen wichtig ist, neben der Arbeit auch einen angemessenen Ausgleich zu haben. Arbeitgeber haben, nicht zuletzt durch die vermutete Leistungssteigerung und erhöhte Zufriedenheit durchaus Verständnis für solche Ansinnen und fördern sie tlw. sogar.[10]

Zu bedenken ist in diesem Kontext zum ersten, ob und wie spezifisch theologische Überlegungen Relevanz für solche Vergemeinschaftungsformen haben, sowie ob und wie zum zweiten Religion zur Produktion von Vergemeinschaftung von Bedeutung ist. Vorstellungen, Prinzipien und Utopien von Vergemeinschaftung bedürfen der kulturellen bzw. rationalen Interpretation, welche sich wiederum im weltanschaulichen Rahmen von Menschen bewegen. Insofern wird die Veränderung des *ideologischen Hintergrunds* einer Gesellschaft auch zu einer veränderten Interpretation von Vergemeinschaftungsformen führen.[11]

Für einen theologischen Beitrag zum Diskurs um Vergemeinschaftungsformen ist dabei die Feststellung wesentlich, dass die Debatte darum inzwischen fest in mundane Zusammenhänge verwoben ist und auch über diese reproduziert wird. Dazu kommt, dass Kirchen und ihnen wohlgesinnte öffentliche Entscheidungsträger die gleichberechtigte Pluralität religiöser und weltlicher Wertsetzung anzuerkennen haben.[12]

10 Vgl. Th. Eggensperger, Freizeit und Muße. Zwischen Zeitsouveränität und Individualisierung, in: Th. Dienberg / Th. Eggensperger / U. Engel (Hrsg.), Auf der Suche nach einem neuen „Wir". Theologische Beiträge zu Gemeinschaft und Individualisierung, Münster 2016, 171–188.

11 Vgl. B. Kohl, O tempora, o mores. Führt das Phänomen der Säkularisierung zu einem Werteverfall?, in: Wort und Antwort 54 (2013), 62–67.

12 T. Gensicke, Jugend und Religiosität, in: Shell Deutschland Holding (Hrsg.), Jugend 2006. Eine pragmatische Generation unter Druck, Frankfurt/M. 2006, 203–239, hier 239.

6. Zusammenfassende Thesen

1. Religion und Religiosität verschwinden nicht, sondern geraten in den Raum des Privaten und werden damit zunehmend unsichtbar. Religion wird zur Privatsache, rückt aber angesichts der tagespolitischen Ereignisse immer wieder in den Focus der öffentlichen Debatte.
2. Es bilden sich für den Einzelnen neue Zugehörigkeitsmodelle aus, so das „Multiple Religious Belonging“ und ein „Multiple Social Belonging“. Es ist allgemein ein Wunsch nach neuen Formen von Gemeinschaft festzustellen.
3. Einer Sphäre des Mundanen eignet das *Zwischen*, in dem Menschen sich interpersonal und sozial koordinieren, gleich welcher religiösen oder weltanschaulichen Grundeinstellung sie verhaftet sind. Eindeutige Zuschreibungen sind hinsichtlich der multiplen religiösen oder sozialen Zugehörigkeit gar nicht mehr möglich.
4. Zu bedenken ist, ob und wie spezifisch theologische Überlegungen Relevanz für die neuen Vergemeinschaftungsformen haben, sowie ob und wie dabei Religion zur Produktion von Vergemeinschaftung von Bedeutung ist.

Thomas Eggensperger / Bernhard Kohl

Research Paper: Society

1. Situation

Currently we observe the following currents in Europe going into opposite directions.

1.1. Traditional Forms of Generating Community vanish

Traditional *forms of generating community* [*Vergemeinschaftungsformen*] change within society (e.g. marriage and family on the micro level; the EU on the macro level), the Church (e.g. parishes); they change or get weaker or fall apart. This also affects religious orders and congregations.

To describe these developments, Michael Hardt and Antonio Negri coined the term "anthropological exodus".[1] They use this term for new forms of life that are, as they phrase it, "totally unable to adapt to family life, to the discipline of plant workers, to the regulation of traditional expression of sexuality, etc." Even if this is some sort of exaggeration, they developed a technical term that is quite useful to categorize a fair amount of contemporary tendencies. The term "Exodus" denotes an intentional exit, a departure that has consequences and ramifications for those who leave as well as for the community that they leave behind. This does not necessarily involve spatial wanderings – that still play a role and will play a roll given the current situation of refugees – but it can also be a

1 Cf. M. Hardt / A. Negri, Empire. Die neue Weltordnung, Frankfurt/M. / New York 2002, 227.

movement in the metaphorical sense and refer to an 'exodus into the inners'.[2]

Examples for those metaphorical and engaged departures, with regards to an existential dimension, are very frequent in post-traditional forms of generating community:

1.2 Post-traditional Forms of Generating Community increase

At the same time, there are new post-traditional forms of generating community that include urban communes, schools that are self-regulating, Childrens' shops, occupied houses, agrarian projects that are oriented towards a subsidiary structure, Sub-economies that are autonomously organized such as swap-meets, renting shops, urban gardening, experiments with polysexuality and polyamory, annexation and repurposing of urban spaces – from guerilla gardening and guerilla knitting to occupy-movements, and last but not least, religiously motivated experiments.

However, these practices are not just wild expressions of protest but have massive theoretical foundations: from a theory of direct democracy, a mutualistic ideal of reciprocal help and ecological sustainability to models of economic solidarity.

This increase of post-traditional forms of generating community is not limited to individual cities or states or countries but has reached the metropolises of many western countries. It is remarkable that the experiments of post-traditional forms of generating community are no longer initiated by mega-organizations (i. e. political parties, unions, churches), but that they form as spontaneous grass-roots movements for a limited time and in individual responsibility. In addition to that, they often also have a distinct spiritual orientation.

2 Cf. D. Loik, Stichwort: Exodus. Leben jenseits von Staat und Konsum?, in: WestEnd 1 (2014), 61–66, here 61.

2. Implications

The changes in the forms of generating community feature some interesting implications[3]:

- They insist that even within capitalist societies there is the possibility of establishing non- or post-capitalist clearings or heterotopias.
- From a utopian theory standpoint, one can conclude that negatory criticism strategies are renounced, which imposes a kind of aniconism on any attempt to imagine alternate forms of community. Rather, any alternate forms of cohabitation are to be discussed immediately, evaluated and revised without anyone expecting a major societal breach.
- New forms of generating community are not blind with regards to theory but they suffer the burden of proof – based on morality as well as a institutional theory: They want to show that alternate forms of communal life present real opportunities for change without breaching into radical social transformation, that they are stable and do work.
- In an ethical perspective, they renew the seemingly Aristotelian attempt to connect the moral right with the experience of bliss. However, they do not base it on a concept of asceticism but rather try to offer an attractive model of live that appeals to the individual.
- Because post-traditional forms of generating community do not require the appropriation of the state nor winning the majority of the discourse in the population, it is able to allow a gradual positioning, an "as well as" or just ask for a binary choice, an "either / or".

3 Cf. ibid. 61–63.

3. Complications

There are some reservations as to post-traditional forms of generating community that are expressed in their understanding as a strategy of resignation and escapism or as a questionable result of the urge for individualism and authenticity. Those reservations are[4]:

- A classical criticism of post-traditional forms of generating community is that they underestimate the ability for integration of traditional forms of generating community and thus – at best – appear inefficient or – at worst – ideological, because they divert attention from the necessity of a universal societal change or from the necessity of a pan-societal consensus.
- An important problem as to the theory of democracies and a somewhat de-politicizing tendency is discovered in the fact that post-traditional forms of generating community do not engage in a critical discourse with society, state and institutions whose children they are, and hence renounce the participation in the public discourse.
- Finally, these practices seem to implode on a regular base due to over-investing in personal relationships. Symptoms of such erosion are often the over-stressing of intimate relationships, being overwhelmed, emotional burnout, personalizing, and moralizing of conflicts.

What now does this pluralizing of forms of life and relationship mean? What is the significance of alternative forms of economy or a partial exodus out of order and organization of society for the connectedness of human beings within such a society?

4 Cf. ibid. 63s.

4. Perspectives

There are three larger trends within society that need to be evaluated:

4.1. Individualization

The process of individualization emphasizes the autonomy of the individual. The development of self-determining forms of lives opens up a whole plethora of new *options*. These compete with *ligatures* that traditionally and institutionally guarantee cohesion. Where these forces of cohesion are missing, the mechanisms of exclusions will gain strength (e. g. national / nationalist demarcation against fugitives, against *Islam* as such, privatizing of consecrated life, distance within ecclesiastic life).[5]

For religion and the Church, this development has consequences: Religion and religiosity do not vanish but migrate into the sphere of the private and become invisible. Religion becomes a private matter.[6]

4.2. Pluralization

In the Europe's late-modernist societies there are tendencies towards pluralism that are rapidly spreading. This concerns mainly forms and styles of life: extra-marital forms of living together, single parents, intentionally being single, same-sex domestic partnerships and marriages, long-distance relationships and marriages intentionally without children. Add to that a new cultural and religious variety of communal life introduced by migration. Clear long-term identifications

5 Cf. Th. Eggensperger, Individualisierung in der Moderne. Alternativentwurf zu einem Verständnis von Säkularisierung als Folge der Modernisierung, in: Th. Dienberg / Th. Eggensperger / U. Engel (Hrsg.), Säkulare Frömmigkeit. Theologische Beiträge zu Säkularisierung und Individualisierung, Münster 2013, 105–107.

6 Cf. J. Casanova, Europäische Säkularisierung auf globaler vergleichender Perspektive. Diagnose und Antwort, in: Th. Dienberg / Th. Eggensperger / U. Engel (Hrsg./Eds.), Himmelwärts und weltgewandt. Kirche und Orden in (post-)säkularer Gesellschaft / Heavenward and Worldly. Church and Religious Orders in (Post) Secular Society, Münster 2014, Münster 2014, 41–54.

(e. g. native or immigrant for 2nd or 3rd generation immigrants) are questioned or dissolve. It is increasingly difficult to make decisions due to increased diversity.

The mega-trend 'Pluralization' doesn't stop at religion either. Hence, for the individual there are now new models of belonging such as "Multiple Religious Belonging" (i. e. at the same time belonging to several, doctrinally competing religions and denominations).[7]

Even more so, it makes sense to differentiate further and not just talk about a multiple religious belonging but a "Multiple Social Belonging" [*English in the original*] since the multitude of belonging does not limit itself to the religious in the strict sense of the word. Religion, Weltanschauung and affinities with regards to specific groups often are co-existing.

Furthermore, in the beginning of the 21st century, there is a longing for new forms of community. This longing however is often missing experience (e. g. in One-Child-Families) and they are highly individualized in public conception. Thus society today is practically no longer an ontological factor that serves personal affirmation but has to be earned socially over and over again with individual effort.[8]

4.3. The Mundane

With regards to the tapestry of human relationships and points of view, it becomes increasingly implausible to separate the political from the religious or the secular. The visibility of these designations has changed so that, although they seem to vanish in the area of the private, they continue to exist but are no longer visible in the public. Here again, it seems to be the easiest to renew our understanding of the sphere or space in order to be able to adequately position the attributes of the politic, the religious, and the secular.

7 Cf. M. Kalsky, Flexibel geloven. Zingeving voorbij de grenzen van religies, Vught 2014.

8 Cf. B. Kohl, Die Anerkennung des Verletzbaren. Eine Rekonstruktion der negativen Hermeneutik der Gottesebenbildlichkeit über die Anerkennungstheorien Axel Honneths und Judith Butlers und über die Theologie Edward Schillebeeckx', Würzburg 2017 (im Druck).

A designation such as "post-secular" will fall short because it does not indicate something new but refers to something following something already existing. This underestimates the "new" of creating the anthropological and sociological network of the space that can no longer be separated into private or public. As an alternative, we suggest to introduce the "sphere of the mundane". The mundane (*mundus* = world) is very congruent with the politic and the public, and even with the secular without being taken by separations and limitations that would not give due respect to the human situation. The Sphere of the Mundane features the *In-between* in which human beings coordinate themselves interpersonally and socially no matter what religious complexion or Weltanschauung they adhere to – all the more since in the wake of multiple religious and social belongings clear delineations are no longer possible.[9]

5. Socio-ethical considerations

The new forms of generating community presented above form for the very reason to (again) experience and live the community of human beings that adhere for more reasons than just economy. Increasingly, employees look for adequate forms of guaranteed relaxation ("Work-Life-Balance", "Sabbatical" [*English in the Original*]) from their work because it is important to them to have an appropriate counterbalance to their work life. For reasons of increase in employee productivity and satisfaction, employers actually appreciate this request and often even support it.[10]

In this context, it is important to keep in mind, firstly, if and how specific theological considerations have relevance for these forms of generating community as well as secondly, if and how religion holds any relevance in generating community. Concepts, principles and

9 Cf. Th. Eggensperger, Individualisierung und die Sphäre des Mundanen, in: Th. Dienberg / Th. Eggensperger / U. Engel (Hrsg./Eds.), Himmelwärts und weltgewandt / Heavenward and worldly, a. a. O., 247–254.

10 Cf. Th. Eggensperger, Freizeit und Muße. Zwischen Zeitsouveränität und Individualisierung, in: Th. Dienberg / Th. Eggensperger / U. Engel (Hrsg.), Auf der Suche nach einem neuen „Wir". Theologische Beiträge zu Gemeinschaft und Individualisierung, Münster 2016, 171–188.

utopias of generating community require cultural or rather rational interpretation that will move within the Weltanschauung's frame of human understanding. This is why a change within the ideological background of a society will change its interpretation of forms of generating community as well.[11]

Essential for a theological contribution to a discourse about forms of generating community is the understanding that the discourse related to it is by now intertwined with mundane contexts and will be reproduced by going through them. Furthermore, churches and those how are their benefactors and public decision makers need to acknowledge the emancipated plurality of religious and mundane value determination.[12]

6. Summarizing Statements:

1. Religion and religiosity do not vanish but are transferred to the sphere of the private and become increasingly invisible. Religion morphs into a private matter but due to contemporary events will be pushed into the focus of public discourse.
2. New models of belonging develop for the use of the individual such as "Multiple Religious Belonging" and a "Multiple Social Belonging". Generally, there is a demand for new forms of community.
3. The Sphere of the Mundane features the *In-between* in which human beings coordinate themselves interpersonally and socially no matter what religious complexion or Weltanschauung they adhere to. In the wake of multiple religious and social belongings clear delineations are no longer possible.
4. It is important to keep in mind if and how specific theological considerations have relevance for new forms of generating community as well as if and how religion holds any relevance in generating community.

11 Cf. B. Kohl, O tempora, o mores. Führt das Phänomen der Säkularisierung zu einem Werteverfall?, in: Wort und Antwort 54 (2013), 62–67.

12 T. Gensicke, Jugend und Religiösität, in: Shell Deutschland Holding (Hrsg.), Jugend 2006. Eine pragmatische Generation unter Druck, Frankfurt/M. 2006, 203–239, here 239.

Ángel Méndez Montoya

Embracing the "Mundane"

I am deeply honored by the invitation to join this roundtable with Bernhard Kohl and Thomas Eggensperger, focusing on a quest for a new "we", with reflections emerging from the particular context of Europe today. This quest is also worldwide. Given that it is a global quest, an immense variety of contexts and horizons are involved: some are comparable, while others may be in contrast. Emerging articulations and practices of a sense of a new "we" may even arise. I am here speaking as a Latin American theologian, so I will mainly focus on theological implications, or provocations of this quest for a new "we". As my discerning voice comes from a Latin American context –more precisely from Mexico– I hope that my response adds an intercontinental ingredient to this dialogue.

Kohl and Eggensperger bring to mind Hardt and Negri's notion of "anthropological exodus". This notion can help us understand the increasing multiple shifts taking place within societies in Europe, and, I may add, in most of the world. This notion is not only literal, but also metaphoric, for it implies shifts in the *Weltanschauung*, transforming multiple forms of social, cultural, political, and religious environments and practices.

One cannot help but think about both the literal and the metaphoric exodus that migrants experience worldwide on a daily basis. In Latin America, this sense of exodus prevails, as more and more individuals and groups move away not only from their original territories, but also from traditional forms of living. These intensified migrations demonstrate new post-traditional "forms of generating community" [*Vergemeinschaftungsformen*] emerging from individuals, societies, and communities. In the USA, for instance, where there are approximately 55 million Latinos/Latinas, these new forms of generating community display an interesting tapestry of cultural, social, political, and religious hybrids. Latin American societies are not monolithic but rather quite diverse. Therefore, communities of Latinos/Latinas living in the USA –whether for a long or short time– undergo many sorts of literal and metaphoric exoduses, and inevitably generate new forms of community. Mexico is a territory of an intense and cruel exodus. Everyday thousands of people migrate from Central and South American countries with the hope of crossing "to the other side" of the Mexican border. Just focusing on the Mexican population living in the USA, a polyphony of "we" becomes clear: some may have been born in the USA, while others may have just arrived with the plan to live there on a more permanent basis; some may be residents, while others may be undocumented; some may come from urban areas, whereas others may come from rural areas; some may be there willingly, while others may be escaping from violence and death threats; some may already speak English, whereas others only Spanish or an indigenous language. The immense variety of people labeled "Mexican-Americans" in the USA makes it difficult to grasp this label's complexity of meanings. Likewise, as it is with every person labeled "Latino/Latina" in the USA, the identity of a "we" that is experienced and practiced by "Mexican-Americans" displays myriad social significations, as well as many post-traditional forms of emerging communities.

Moreover, because it is indeed difficult to clearly delineate the boundaries between the private and the public, and between the secular and the religious, I appreciate the notion of "the mundane" that Kohl and Eggensperger suggest using in order to grasp the complexities of the emergence of a new "we". Societies in today's world shed light on the in-betweenness of the mundane: the co-implication of categories such as the private and the public, the religious and the secular. The mundane also describes the in-between space linking the cultural, social, political and religious spheres. The mundane alludes to the porosity of the boundaries separating the diverse expressions of social life. Given that this in-between space is liquid, co-implicating and under constant transformation, the mundane gives voice to society's new engagements with the world. This sense of worldly or planetary engagement is rapidly intensifying as globalization and virtual networks permeate the warp and weft of daily life. Furthermore, as explained by Kohl and Eggensperger, these social interactions construct new trends of belonging, such as individualization and pluralization, creating impersonal as well as interpersonal interactions with the mundane. For sure, this also isolates and ghettoizes groups of people, creating subaltern societies, leaving people rejected, a multiplicity of individuals in the periphery of society. As in Europe, in Latin America the mundane also expresses new forms of community, new "exoduses", and emerging forms of social connectivity.

The implications and complications of these new forms of generating community are certainly massive. Kohl and Eggensperger provide various examples of some implications and complications in today's world, which go from emancipatory to violent or destructive social practices and patterns, and also, from pluralizing to individualizing engagements with the mundane. Speaking as a theologian, this social reality definitely incites theological thinking. Without minimizing the great challenges ahead of us, I would like to concentrate on some opportunities for theology, which could be provoked by these new forms of generating community. Provocation shakes us up, incites us to take action, and makes us move beyond our comfort zone, or the status quo. Provocation may shake us from apathy and indifference. At the heart of the Capuchin Franciscan and Dominican religious traditions, I believe this engagement with the mundane must not be left behind, and most particularly as our religious communities inevitably undergo this sense of a new "we".

Again, to focus on opportunities does not imply minimizing the challenges ahead of us, for they are certainly overwhelming, as the world undergoes a greater rise of waves of fundamentalism, and myriad expressions of supremacy, xenophobia, misogyny, and homophobia. Yet, both Francis of Assisi and Dominic de Guzmán may encourage us not to flee and hide in our monasteries, but to embrace the world with courage and hope, to engage the mundane with a critical, prophetic, and transformative presence. Do let's recall that they both also lived in a rapidly shifting world, in which worldviews were collapsing, while new patterns of social interaction were emerging. Francis of Assisi and Dominic de Guzmán ultimately took all these liquid social realities as opportunities to "incarnate" God among us.

I propose considering the following four opportunities that I believe the mundane incites theologians and religious communities to meditate on. My purpose is not to theologize the mundane, but quite the opposite: to critically see how the mundane provokes a theological thinking that encourages a greater engagement with the mundane, and empowers communities to work together in favor of the common good, caring for those without agency, those lacking recognition. Without a doubt, there are more opportunities beyond these four brief suggestions. Therefore, I hope that my own response to Kohl and Eggensperger may provoke a dialogue and shared thinking about many possible strategies as part of the quest for a new "we".

1. Christian theology must embrace the mundane, for God is in the mundane just as much as God is elsewhere. The theological provocation arising from the mundane is that theology must not be indifferent to the immanent world. Fleeing the world has brought about a long history of theology and religious practices tending to "spiritualize" God and the world to such an extent that they are oblivious to people's lives; or this spiritualizing agenda is used in order to justify fear, rejection, and apathy towards the mundane. God is inscribed in the mundane, and this incites a critical theological reflection to discern upon the in-betweenness of the divine's presence and absence in our midst. By virtue of envisioning God's incarnation and self-involvement within the narrative of creation, the mundane may incite a resistance to narrow the world down to a homogenizing reality, and so learn from a complex *Weltanschauung*, from the heterogeneous in-between space where divine and human agency are interwoven.

2. If God is paradoxically both the mundane and the ultimate Other, this may incite a discernment upon how "we" and "they" are constructed in today's world, and how it enables us or not to resonate with the ethical stance of the "*for you*" of God. With regard to Jesus's presentation of the divine embracing the mundane, the narrative of Matthew 25 could shed some light on the figure of God embracing and identifying with the "other". We cannot deny that God invites to continue generating communities of multiple "we's". But at times, the perils of socially identifying with a "we" could construct rigid and abusive social interactions (as Jesus so well noted in his own times) that often colonize and ghettoize the "other", those who are not part of the "we". The other is seen as a threat to traditional forms of life in social circles, and often the other is taken as a scapegoat to preserve hegemonic and violent traditions. Sadly, there are times when religious communities tend to enclose themselves to the extent

of constructing a sense of a hegemonic, "colonizing we" incapable of recognizing the other. The huge economic and geopolitical divide between the Northern and Southern hemispheres only reveals the peak of the iceberg of the hegemonic block of the most privileged sectors dominating the most vulnerable people in the world. With the inauguration of the Donald Trump era, there has been an intensification of the tendency for societies and religious communities to build visible and invisible walls, unaware of and indifferent to the other, even destroying them. Jesus's identifying God embracing those who are in the periphery of society, provokes a discernment about the need for a "decolonizing theology", so that it enables and empowers practices of inclusion, dialogue, and care for those who are in the diaspora, beyond the walls of the "we". This also implies an opportunity for a greater dialogue and engagement with religious traditions beyond the rigid walls of Christianity. Are we willing to take this opportunity that comes from these new forms of generating community and undergo a "decolonizing theological exodus", even if this implies walking in the midst of a literal and metaphorical diaspora?

3. The biblical narratives often symbolize the act of encountering God in diasporic spaces, in the periphery of the visible and invisible walls of society, or in the figure of the foreigner, the alien other. This is particularly the case within many biblical narratives where God is encountered among both literal and metaphoric migrations, and upon meeting the foreigner. Indeed, migration, diaspora, and exodus are paradigmatic in Jesus's own narrative and vocation: the divine migrating into the flesh of the mundane; a prophetic presence speaking from a social, religious, and political diaspora; inciting an exodus, moving away from a dynamic of violence, death, and scapegoating, transitioning into another time and space under the imaginary and the living practice of peace, inclusion, and mutual caring. Jesus experienced all sorts of migrations or exoduses, and even an ideological exodus. Recall Mt 15, 21–28, when a foreigner, a Canaanite woman, cried out to Jesus in public, asking him for a miracle for her daughter who was severely oppressed by a demon. Jesus replied from a "we" position defined by privilege, supremacy, and exclusion. So, he told her, "It's not right to take the children's bread and throw it to the dogs." His relationship to her clearly delineated the social

and religious boundaries between "we" and "they", between insiders and outsiders, between men and women, between upper and lower classes, between the truly human and those people who are "animals." Not only was she a foreigner, but she was also a woman. And in the patriarchal society in which Jesus grew up, women were treated as subaltern subjects. So "dog" is a label used to refer to foreigners; but here it also becomes a double label, for she is a woman, she who "is" a "dog". Her presence is provoking for Jesus and his disciples (who earlier encouraged Jesus to ignore her and send her away). The Canaanite woman broke the social boundaries, crying out in a public space, and approaching a public male figure. Jesus's reply certainly could be seen as the reaction of someone who is provoked, voicing the social and religious supremacy of an exclusionary tradition. Or perhaps Jesus was unmasking the absurd violence of the "we". Either way, she was not silenced by bigotry. And so she sent Jesus her final and most direct provocation. She said, "Yes, Lord. But even the dogs eat the crumbs that fall from their masters' tables." I tend to imagine that at this moment, Jesus broadened his own ideological *Weltanschauung*, and it was he who first received the miracle of the understanding provided by this woman. It was he who first received transformation, which then moved him to tell her, after finally acknowledging her, in total surprise and astonishment, "Oh woman! Great is your faith." The miracle was granted, but Jesus first had to disentangle the knots of his own and his social groups' supremacist confinement of a "we". And who are the "dogs" of today's society, those "we" do not acknowledge, and look down at? It is those without agency living in the periphery who are the unworthy dogs not invited to take a place at the table: women, people in the LGBTI communities, migrants, the disabled, the poor. Mexico has become notorious for its human rights crisis. On a daily basis, many women, homosexuals, transsexuals, and migrants are harassed, tortured, raped, and murdered. Here again, the mundane provokes us to open our eyes to see and recognize those who are made invisible, or are only visible as subaltern subjects. Just like Jesus was provoked by this Canaanite woman, may "we" (first of all theologians, and brothers and sisters in religious communities) be willing to let ourselves be provoked by the dogs of society, those who eat the crumbs falling from the masters' table.

4. The planet is also part of a collective "we". The planet is in the mundane, as the mundane is in the planet. In his Encyclical letter, Pope Francis called the planet "our common home," for, echoing Saint Francis' canticle of creation, the Earth is a common "sister" and "mother" that requires special praise and care. Because "nothing in this world is indifferent to us," we must not be indifferent to our wounded Earth that cries out for help:

> *This sister now cries out to us because of the harm we have inflicted on her by our irresponsible use and abuse of the goods with which God has endowed her. We have come to see ourselves as her lords and masters, entitled to plunder her at will. The violence present in our hearts, wounded by sin, is also reflected in the symptoms of sickness evident in the soil, in the water, in the air and in all forms of life. This is why the earth herself, burdened and laid waste, is among the most abandoned and maltreated of our poor; she "groans in travail" (Rom 8:22). We have forgotten that we ourselves are dust of the earth (cf. Gen 2:7); our very bodies are made up of her elements, we breathe her air and we receive life and refreshment from her waters (Papal Encyclical Laudato Si, 2).*

The Earth cries out similarly to what we heard earlier about the Canaanite woman in Matthew's Gospel, who cried out for Jesus's help, thus provoking a response. "We have come to see ourselves as her lords and masters, entitled to plunder her at will." Sadly, we are the masters seated at the table, eating the bread that the earth gives us, while the earth is a dog that eats the crumbs falling from our table. We cannot remain unmoved, indifferent to a maltreated planet. We must be incited to materialize concrete transformations in order to collectively set up a healing relationship with our micro and macro ecological environments, our common home. Finding a common "we" that includes the planet is a great challenge. The planet's wellbeing should be a common concern, even beyond the walls of Christian communities, and religious institutions, indeed, of the fully mundane realm. This planetary reality is also an opportunity to lovingly and ethically embrace the planet, since it also inspires the quest for a "we" that does not allow us to become indifferent to this world.

* * *

Zusammenfassung zu: Ángel Méndez Montoya, Die Umarmung des Mundanen

Ángel Méndez Montoya (México Ciudad | Mexiko) nähert sich der Suche nach einem *neuen Wir* dezidiert von seinem lateinamerikanischen Hintergrund aus an. Er konstatiert, dass der von Hardt und Negri eingebrachte Begriff des *anthropologischen Exodus* inzwischen weltweit zutreffe und auf die vielfältigen Veränderungen der sozialen, kulturellen, politischen und religiösen Praktiken und Umgebungen hinweise, die sich derzeit global beobachten lassen.

Insbesondere Migranten erleben diesen Exodus in einem wörtlichen aber auch in einem metaphorischen Sinn, da sie ihre Heimat nicht nur räumlich verlassen, sondern damit auch ihre Lebensformen und Gewohnheiten, wodurch neue kulturelle, soziale, politische und religiöse Hybridformen des „Wir" entstehen. Für diese Formen ist der Terminus des *Mundanen* eine passende Beschreibung, da er das Dazwischen-Sein, die Durchlässigkeit der Grenzen zwischen privat und öffentlich, säkular und religiös erfasst. Außerdem ergeben sich durch den Terminus vier Anstöße für eine theologische Reflektion: 1.) Das Mundane ist ein locus theologicus, da Gott im Mundanen ebenso präsent ist, wie überall sonst auch. 2.) Wenn Gott sowohl im Mundanen als auch im absolut Anderen präsent ist, dann können daraus Schlussfolgerungen für Konstruktionen des „Wir" und des „Ihr" gezogen werden. 3.) Biblisch wird Gott häufig in Grenzsituationen erfahrbar. Dadurch werden Menschen, die sich in solchen Situationen befinden zum Ort der Gotteserfahrung. 4.) Der Planet Erde ist Teil eines kollektiven „Wir". Dadurch ist die Erde das Mundane, genauso, wie das Mundane die Erde ist, da auf ihr nichts existiert, was sich indifferent zur Menschheit verhielte.

Karl Heinz Knubel

Wenn es *besser* werden soll, muss es *anders* werden!

Vor mir liegt ein Thesenpapier, Verfasser sind Bernhard Kohl und Thomas Eggensperger. Ich darf einige Bemerkungen zum Papier machen und bedanke mich bei Thomas Dienberg, der mich „aus heiterem Himmel" – ein sehr passendes Wortbild – dazu gefragt hat.

Ein Teil-Projekt, dem sich die Verfassergemeinschaft unter der General-Überschrift „Auf der Suche nach einem neuen Wir" gewidmet hat, heißt „Gesellschaft". Ein *Projekt* entsteht, oder auch nicht, wenn es ein Problem gibt, dessen Lösung man sich zuwenden möchte; das setzt aber voraus, dass das Problem als solches erkannt wird. So wie ein Ort, zu dem ein Wanderer unterwegs ist, ist das über verschiedene Wege denkbar, denn „viele Wege führen nach Rom". Dem Teil-Projekt „Gesellschaft" nähert sich das Thesenpapier in klassischer Weise: Beschreibung, denkbare Entwicklungen, Abwägungen, zusammenfassende Betrachtung.

Wer ein Buch liest, ist häufig der Versuchung ausgesetzt, am Ende anzufangen – bei Kriminalromanen eine Standardversuchung. Meine Antwort auf das Thesenpapier fängt am Ende an. Da heißt es: „Religion und Religiosität verschwinden nicht, sondern geraten in den Raum des Privaten und werden damit zunehmend unsichtbar." Ist diese Aussage eine richtige Beschreibung des Problems, dem man sich zuwendet, oder ist sie zunächst einmal schön geredet? Kann man Religion und Religiosität und deren Probleme weltweit sehen, und sind sie nicht hier bei uns *doch* im Verschwinden begriffen und nicht nur abgetaucht? Machen sich die Verfasser das Problem mit einer solchen Feststellung nicht doch zu leicht, legen es nur ab in einem Regal, um es bei Gelegenheit wieder heraus zu holen, oder auch nicht? Auch sollten wir nicht davon ausgehen, es gäbe das eben genannte Problem des Verschwindens von Religion als *globales* Problem, dem man sich auch global zuwenden kann; es gibt kein globales Problem, nicht einmal der Klimawandel ist ein globales Problem: *hier* leidet man unter einer „Jahrhundert-Dürre“, und dort stehen ganze Landesteile unter Wasser, hier zeigt ein Plakat eine Schale mit einer Handvoll Reis darin mit der Inschrift „Weniger wäre leer“, und woanders widmen sich ganze Staaten dem Problem des Übergewichts ihrer Bürger. Wer will, kann mit globalen Überschriften oder Zusammenfassungen arbeiten, die Lösungen oder Lösungsvorschläge können jedoch immer nur regionale sein.

Religion braucht Stabilität, braucht Verlässlichkeit und braucht Gemeinschaft, das ist zwar ein anderes Thema, aber es passt zum Konzept der Verfasser dieses Papiers, sich mit dem Verschwinden von Religion, dem Entstehen neuer Gemeinschaften und neuer Formen von Gemeinschaften zu befassen. Dabei müssen wir sehen, dass so etwas beim Einzelnen anfängt, der sich zunächst einmal nicht so sehr die neue Gemeinschaft, sondern viel mehr seine eigenen Interessen, *seine* Sichtweisen und *deren* Verwirklichungen vornimmt. Da sind die zuvor genannten Begriffe wie Verlässlichkeit, Stabilität, auch Instanz und Klugheit eher Worte aus einem fremden Vokabular.

Dann heißt es im Thesenpapier; „Was bedeutet aber nun eine solche Pluralisierung von Lebens- und Beziehungsformen“, und gefragt wird im Zusammenhang mit erwarteten Komplikationen, „was bedeutet ein Ausstieg aus Ordnung und Organisation für den Zusammenhalt von Menschen innerhalb einer solchen Gesellschaft?“ Ein Aussteigen setzt voraus, dass ein alternativer Zusammenschluss in neuen Formen aus individueller Sicht wünschenswert oder sogar erforderlich sein muss. Für eine Anzahl von Individuen ist das denkbar, aber selbst eine beachtliche Menge von „Du s“ ist noch kein „Wir“, und nicht einmal „Du und ich“ sind von vorneherein schon ein „Wir“.

Wenn im Punkt 6.3 der Zusammenfassung die Rede ist von der „Sphäre des Mundanen“, und von „verhaftet“ sein, dann sind das Paradoxa: im „Mundanen“ ist man eben *nicht* verhaftet, man steigt ein und steigt wieder aus wie bei einer Straßenbahn „hopp on – hopp off“, und wenn das auch nur ein Minimum von Stabilität hat, nimmt man vielleicht gerade mal eine Weile Platz: es gibt keine Verpflichtungen oder Bindungen, allenfalls Zugehörigkeiten, die jederzeit neu definiert werden können; weder ein Einstieg noch eine Aufkündigung setzt Formalitäten voraus, nur ein Tun. Und darum ist es gewagt, solch einem Tun einen einrahmenden und dazu noch kaum verstehbaren Namen zu geben.

Ein Kernsatz des Thesenpapiers heißt: „Zu bedenken ist, ob und wie spezifisch theologische Überlegungen Relevanz haben für die neuen Vergemeinschaftungsformen, sowie, ob und wie dabei Religion zur Produktion von Vergemeinschaftung von Bedeutung ist." Wenn so formuliert wird, geht es eben doch um weltweite Überlegungen, um weltweite Bedeutung, denn die Religion, um die es *hier* geht, *ist* weltweit und nicht örtlich beschränkt auf ein Tal im Schwarzwald. Kann man überhaupt der Religion eine „Produktion" zutrauen, und muss uns nicht ein Wort „Vergemeinschaftungsform" schon aus Gründen des Sprachgefühls stören? „Gemeinschaft" will eben doch einen Zugehörigkeitswillen und auf Dauer sogar gesellschaftliche Akzeptanz und auch öffentliche Stützung.

Wenn man auf der letzten Seite des Thesenpapiers angefangen ist, heißt das nicht, dass nicht schon vorher auf jeder Seite viele und sehr bedenkenswerte Überlegungen stehen, allerdings in einer Sprache, die zwar jedem Anspruch auf Wissenschaftlichkeit sehr gerecht wird, sich aber fragen lassen muss, ob sie von den „Suchenden nach einem neuen Wir" überhaupt verstanden wird?

So viel als *Antwort* zum Thesenpapier. Darf ich bitte noch etwas sagen, das nach meiner Meinung zu unserem Zusammensein passt, ohne dass Sie mir hinterher vorwerfen, ich hätte mich doch zu sehr mit Oberflächlichem oder mit Dingen beschäftigt, die nicht zum Thema gehören. Adressat wäre hier möglicherweise das Thesenpapier „Kirche" und meine Antwort wäre eine interdisziplinäre, und als solche doch hochgeschätzt in Wissenschaft und Forschung!

Die Bedeutung, der Einfluss der Theologie auf die Bildung neuer Gemeinschaften ist sehr eine Frage nach der Vorgehensweise der Theologen, hier besser gesagt der operativen Kirche. Jede Gemeinschaft ist die Summe ihrer Individuen, und jedes Individuum will dort abgeholt werden, wo es beim beabsichtigten Verlassen der Gemeinschaft wartend steht. Bis heute ist das Individuum im Sprachgebrauch der Amtskirche ein Teil des Kirchenvolkes, der „Gläubigen", der „Herde", oder, wenn es ganz problematisch ausgedrückt wird, ein „Schaf", und das Schaf gehorcht oder hat zu gehorchen dem Hirten, dem Pastor, was nichts anderes heißt, und der „Hirte" freut sich, wenn er ein verlorenes Schaf wieder gefunden hat. Wer sagt bitte der „Kirche", dass das Bild vom Hirten und seiner Herde in hohem Maße untauglich, wahrscheinlich sogar schädlich ist für einen wie auch immer gedachten Neubeginn, für eine, wie auch immer, gedachte Antwort auf das Problem des Abtauchens und, mehr noch, auf das sehr viel Wichtigere des Bleibens?

Wer sagt dem Bischof, dass der Stab, auf den er sich stützt, in seiner Symbolik gerade noch als Stütze verstanden wird, er ist allerdings aus dem Hirtenstab entwickelt, und der war kaum jemals mit Gold ummantelt und mit Edelsteinen verziert, dass aber der *Hut*, die Mitra, die ihn größer macht, und wohl auch größer machen sollte, nicht mehr verstanden wird, so wenig, wie das Tragen der Mitra durch die Messdiener mit behandschuhten Händen, auch nicht die Form der Beweihräucherung im Hochamt, schon gar nicht, wenn sie dem Celebrans dreifach zuteilwird, während das Kirchenvolk, die Drei- oder Vierhundert im Kirchenschiff, sich mit zweifach begnügen darf?

Und: wendet sich der Bischof, der Oberhirte, an seine Herde, dann wird das so lange nicht die gewünschte Wirkung haben, wie nicht der Einzelne erreicht wird, *und nur auf den kommt's an*. Was für eine blasse Wirkung hat doch ein vorgelesener Brief verglichen mit einer Predigt, die nicht vorgelesen sondern gepredigt wird?

Wir sind eben *nicht* da, wo wir heute sein sollten, auch dann nicht, wenn die Zeiten vorbei sind, in denen der Brief an den Herrn Pastor mit der Abkürzung „Hochw." geschmückt wurde. Aber so etwas dürfte *auch* in einem Thesenpapier stehen, das sich mit der Frage beschäftigt, wie es um den Einfluss und die Wirkung theologischer Überlegungen bei der Bildung neuer Gemeinschaften steht, und natürlich auch um die Überlegungen und Botschaften, die sich an die bestehenden, überkommenen Gemeinschaften richten, also an die einzelnen Mitglieder *unserer* Kirche, deren Mitglied ich gerne und mit Überzeugung bin. In der Kirche gehen Botschaften häufig über die Köpfe der Zuhörer hinweg, nicht nur, weil der Priester normalerweise erhöht steht. Die kirchliche Sprache ist eben nicht die Sprache der „Kirche der Armen" und der „Bescheidenheit". Die Kanzel war eben nicht nur der Vorgänger des Mikrofons.

Natürlich denkt die römisch-katholische Kirche in Jahrhunderten, aber das darf nicht dazu führen, dass sie aktuelle Notwendigkeiten, in der Gegenwart auftretende Fragen und Probleme in gleichen Zeitschritten angehen und einer Regelung zuführen darf. Sie ist mit denen, die zu ihr gehören, eine Kirche „*in* der Zeit". Und nur *gemeinsam* sind wir „Kirche", sagt auch das II. Vaticanum. Überzeugungskraft der größten Religionsgemeinschaft der Welt könnte und müsste anders und besser wahrgenommen werden.

Wartet nicht mittlerweile auch der „Gläubige" vor Ort auf irgendwelche erkennbare Zeichen, Veränderungen oder wenigstens Ankündigungen von Veränderungen, dass man fern von Rom die Worte aus Rom gehört und verstanden habe, die von „Bescheidenheit" und von „Kirche der Armen" und von „Barmherzigkeit" sprechen, natürlich besonders in Zeiten von Flüchtlingskrise und Asylantenströmen? „Wir schaffen das!", eine Übersetzung des christlichen „Du sollst Deinen Nächsten lieben wie Dich selbst" in die Sprache unserer Zeit, hat die protestantische Pfarrerstochter gesagt und nicht die katholische Bischofskonferenz. Kann nicht auch die Schlichtheit der protestantischen Geistlichen einschließlich ihrer Bischöfe etwas, wenigstens etwas abfärben auf das Auftreten der römischen Kirche, zumal wenn dies im Fernsehen geschieht?

Das waren jetzt Punkte, Gedanken, Überlegungen, die einen Zusammenhang haben mit dem, was gefragt wurde: „Was können wir tun, wenn wir die Einzelnen, die neuen „Wir s" erreichen wollen, die sich mit Fragen des Austretens aus den bisherigen Gemeinschaften befassen?" Und, wenn gefragt wurde, sind dann nicht auch Antworten gefragt?

Und *noch* etwas, etwas zum Schluss (auch im Thesenpapier steht das Wichtigste ja am Schluss).

Das Thesenpapier *beschreibt* ein Problem, und hat das Beschreiben zu seinem Projekt gemacht. Ist Beschreiben genug, oder wäre doch wohl der eigentliche Zweck, sich im Rahmen eines Projektes mit dem Problem zu befassen *und zu seiner Lösung beizutragen*? Wenn ein „Abtauchen" festgestellt wird, stellt sich dann nicht sofort die Frage nach dem Auftauchen und allen Problemen, die damit verbunden sind? Ist das Beschreiben, auch wenn es sehr in die Tiefe geht, und wenn es das Problem nach allen wissenschaftlichen Regeln in seine problematischen Details zerlegt, schon das, was man erwarten kann? *Mein* Blick auf das Papier ist der eines Kaufmanns, eines Unternehmers. Und als der war ich ständig der Frage ausgesetzt: „Was wollen wir jetzt *tun*?" Sehr oft habe ich dann einen Satz gesagt und mich auch danach gerichtet: „Es wird nicht alles besser, wenn es anders wird, aber, wenn es *besser* werden soll, muss es *anders* werden!" Das hieß, dass ich alle Probleme zielorientiert, und noch deutlicher, *lösungsorientiert* angehen musste.

Das heißt aber auch – hier und heute – ist etwas anders geworden?

Ich bin der Versuchung erlegen, dies alles vor einem Auditorium zu sagen, das sich in viel höheren geistigen und geistlichen Sphären bewegt – wer weiß aber, wann die Gelegenheit wieder kommt?

* * *

Summary: Karl Heinz Knubel, Improving means changing.

Karl Heinz Knubel (Münster | Germany) starts his "re-lecture" by asking whether and to what extent we can consider religion, religiosity and their problems from a global perspective, or whether, in this area as in all others, a "regional perspective" is in fact required. He notes that there are no problems that can be defined globally. For that reason, a view of religion and how it forms communities must initially also be considered regionally, i. e. starting with the individual.

One aspect that Knubel finds problematic is that the modern search for community is first and foremost focused on personal interests, personal views and their realisation, and this runs counter to the need for stability, reliability and continuity in the development of religious communities. Individuals who abandon antiquated forms of the collective do not automatically form a new We. Knubel is therefore critical of the notion of "imprisonment in the worldly", which he considers paradoxical: the individual is not imprisoned or bound by but simply temporarily part of the worldly.

Knubel believes that the potential significance of theology for the formation of new communities depends above all on the approach of the theologians; of the church in practice. The theologians and the church must meet the individual on the point of leaving the community; meet the individual where he or she stands and waits for humility, for a church of the poor and for a translation of "Love thy neighbour as thyself" into the language of our time.

Michaela Pfadenhauer

Techniken der Zugehörigkeit zu posttraditionalen Gemeinschaften

1. Einleitung

G*esellschaften* heute werden soziologisch insbesondere prozesshaft beschrieben: Modernisierung, Pluralisierung, Individualisierung, Globalisierung und neuerdings Mediatisierung gelten als Metaprozesse mit gravierenden Konsequenzen in ökonomischen, politischen und kulturellen Kontexten.[1] Ohne deren Tiefendimensionen hier im Einzelnen entfalten zu können, ist deren Meta-Konsequenz, dass sich die bisher dominierenden Klassen- und Schichtstrukturen zunehmend auflösen oder jedenfalls keine soziale Einbindung mehr bieten[2]. Und auch die überall zu beobachtenden ‚Gegenbewegungen' (Regionalismen, Fundamentalismen ebenso wie die von uns beobachtete De-Mediatisierung[3] etc.) ändert nichts an dieser generellen Entwicklungstendenz.

Gleichwohl sind auch Gesellschaften in diesem fortschreitenden Modernisierungsprozess nicht strukturlos. In wirtschaftlichen und politischen Zusammenhängen bilden sich neue Organisations- oder Vergesellschaftungsformen. Und sozio-kulturell entwickeln sich neue Vergemeinschaftungsmuster, die wir als posttraditional[4]

1 Vgl. dazu den Beitrag von Bernhard Kohl und Thomas Eggensperger in diesem Band, 31–39 // 41–48.

2 P. Eisewicht / T. Grenz / M. Pfadenhauer (Hrsg.), Techniken der Zugehörigkeit, Karlsruhe 2012.

3 M. Pfadenhauer, T. Grenz (Hrsg.), De-Mediatisierung. Diskontinuitäten, Non-Linearitäten und Ambivalenzen im Mediatisierungsprozess, 2017.

4 R. Hitzler / A. Honer / M. Pfadenhauer (Hrsg.), Posttraditionale Gemeinschaften. Theoretische und ethnografische Erkundungen, Wiesbaden 2008; R. Hitzler, Posttraditionale Vergemeinschaftung. Über neue Formen der Sozialbindung, in: Berliner Debatte INITIAL 9/1 (1998), 81–89.

bezeichnen und deren wesentliche Kennzeichen im Folgenden entfaltet werden sollen. Sehr allgemein lässt sich sagen, dass deren vergemeinschaftende Kraft nicht mehr aus ähnlichen sozialen Lagen erwächst, die Menschen in Schicksalsgemeinschaften einbindet. Es sind vielmehr ähnliche Lebensziele und ähnliche ästhetische Ausdrucksformen, die Menschen dazu veranlasst, sich zu vergemeinschaften – eine Entwicklung, die in der Sozialstrukturanalyse seit geraumer Zeit nahelegt, die herkömmliche Beschreibung von sozialen Lagen (mittels Klassen- und Schichtmodellen) durch Milieumodelle zu ersetzen, die nicht selten auch in Bezug auf Kirchenzugehörigkeit angewendet werden.

2. Vergemeinschaftung statt Gemeinschaft

Die Diagnose neuer Vergemeinschaftungsmuster ändert erstmal nichts an den für jede Art von Gemeinschaft geltenden Konstitutionsbedingungen: a) die Abgrenzung gegenüber einem wie auch immer gearteten „Nicht-Wir", b) ein wodurch auch immer entstandenes *Zu(sammen)gehörigkeitsgefühl*, c) ein wie auch immer geartetes, von den Mitgliedern der Gemeinschaft geteiltes *Interesse* bzw. *Anliegen*, d) eine wie auch immer geartete, von den Mitgliedern der Gemeinschaft anerkannte *Wertsetzung* und schließlich e) irgendwelche, wie auch immer gearteten, den Mitgliedern zugänglichen *Interaktions(zeit)räume*.

Bereits die von Ferdinand Tönnies 1887 so genannte „Gemeinschaft des Blutes" war von diesem Ahnherr der soziologischen Gemeinschaftsforschung nicht als „naturwüchsig" konnotiert.[5] Tönnies zufolge *kann* sie sich aus der Mutter-Kind-Bindung, aus der Familie und aus der Verwandtschaft heraus entwickeln – das muss aber nicht sein. Die „Gemeinschaft des Blutes" ist also keineswegs identisch gedacht mit natürlichen Verwandtschaftsverhältnissen, sondern erwächst durch den – anthropologisch verstandenen – menschlichen „Wesenswillen" (dies gilt umso mehr für die von Tönnies angedachten Formen der „Gemeinschaft des Ortes" und der „Gemeinschaft des Geistes").

5 F. Tönnies, Gemeinschaft und Gesellschaft, Darmstadt 1979.

Gemeinschaft begreift Tönnies somit als Entsprechung der im Menschen schlechthin verwurzelten Wesensart, mit anderen Menschen auf der Grundlage von emotionalen u. a. Bindungen zusammengehören zu wollen – zweifelhaft ist, ob dieser Wille auf Verlässlichkeit und Dauer angelegt ist. Ausgangspunkt für ein soziologisches Gemeinschaftsverständnis ist also der anthropologische Befund, dass Menschen „von Natur aus" zur Gemeinschaft strebende Wesen: *zoon politicon* sind, was nicht im Widerspruch dazu steht, dass Gemeinschaft, selbst die „des Blutes", ein Kulturprodukt ist, d. h.: eine von Menschen produzierte Gesellungsform, die durch Zeichen, Symbole und Rituale konstituiert, stabilisiert und restituiert wird. Voraussetzung für eine so verstandene, also als Form menschlicher Sozialität verstandene Gemeinschaft sind nicht die für die Existenz biologischer Gemeinschaften verantwortlich gemachten Instinkte, Gene oder Meme, sondern Lebewesen mit Handlungsproblemen; d. h. Wesen, die sich nicht instinktiv verhalten, d. h. die ihr Leben nicht einfach „natürlich" leben können, sondern die es „tätig" produzieren und reproduzieren müssen und dabei ordnungsstiftend(e) Kultur hervorbringen.

Nicht nur bis in die Antike, sondern bis in die Mythen der Archaik lässt sich zurückverfolgen, dass Menschen ihre jeweilige Gemeinschaft auch als kulturell ‚produziert', d. h. als mehr oder weniger explizit durch Menschen oder durch ‚höhere Wesen' gestiftete Sozialform wahrgenommen haben. Typisch für die Moderne und damit relativ jung ist demgegenüber die Auffassung, dass jede Art von Gemeinschaft nicht nur ‚heroisch' oder kollektiv, sondern tatsächlich auch *individuell* re-produziert werden muss, d. h., dass jeder Einzelne ständig zur Aufrechterhaltung, ja zur Konstitution der Gemeinschaft beiträgt. In dem Maße aber, in dem Gemeinschaft dergestalt vom Schicksal zur Aufgabe und Zugehörigkeit zu einer Gemeinschaft zu einer Frage der Entscheidung wird, avancieren auch Fragen nach Aufwand und Ertrag zu Kriterien der individuellen Entscheidung für oder gegen die Zugehörigkeit zu einer Gemeinschaft.

Dieses ökonomische Kalkül, das ein individualisiertes Verhältnis zu Gemeinschaft voraussetzt, ist keineswegs nur für die soziologische Analytikerin, sondern auch für die jeweiligen Akteure selber *als solches* erkennbar. Wenn wir unter den derzeit gegebenen Individualisierungsbedingungen eine Veränderung der *Produktion* von

Gemeinschaften konstatieren (und zwar sowohl tradierter Formen als auch vielfältiger neuer, von uns als ,posttraditional' bezeichneter Formen), dann meinen wir damit die zunehmende *Sichtbarkeit* der *individuell* auf Vorteilsgewinnung gerichteten Produktion von Gemeinschaft.[6]

Die darüber hinaus gehende generelle Diagnose lautet, dass Gemeinschaft ,heute' (*auch*) unter ökonomischen ,Vorzeichen' (wie Absatzmarktstrategien, Ressourcenschöpfung, Gewinnmaximierung usw.) produziert wird, und dass sich beim Aufbau, bei der Stabilisierung und (Re-) Vitalisierung ganz unterschiedlicher Formen von Gemeinschaft sehr direkt ökonomisch interessierte Akteure engagieren. Dies lässt sich empirisch anhand vielfältiger Manifestationen posttraditionaler Vergemeinschaftung zeigen – seien es nun Brand Communities,[7] Jugendszenen[8] oder situative Event-Gemeinschaften,[9] die im Rahmen inszenierter Massenspektakel (wie Paraden, Umzügen, Public Viewing u. v. a. m.) auftreten. Was hier vor sich geht ist eine *wechselseitige* Durchdringung von Kultur und Ökonomie, die als Resultat eines Übergangs von fordistischen zu post-fordistischen Produktions- und Konsumweisen beschrieben wird. Produziert, d. h. zur Verfügung gestellt werden Vergemeinschaftungsgelegenheiten (Interaktionszeiträume) und Vergemeinschaftungs-anzeigen (werthaltige ästhetische Ausdrucksmöglichkeiten), die von den Produzenten (z. B. Unternehmen; Werbe- und Marketingagenturen) ihrerseits wiederum „ökonomisch in Wert gesetzt" werden (müssen).

Eine Reaktion auf diese Entwicklung sind kapitalismuskritische Initiativen, die Entwürfe jenseits der Marketing- und

6 R. Hitzler / M. Pfadenhauer, Die Ökonomisierung der Produktion von Gemeinschaft, in: K.-S. Rehberg (Hrsg.), Die Natur der Gesellschaft. Verhandlungen des 32. Kongresses der Deutschen Gesellschaft für Soziologie in Kassel 2006, Frankfurt/M. 2008, 595–608.

7 M. Pfadenhauer, Netzwerke produktbezogenen Sonderwissens: Markengemeinschaften vs. Aneignungskulturen, in: K. Lichtblau (Hrsg.), Transnationale Vergesellschaftungen. Verhandlungen des 35. Kongresses der Deutschen Gesellschaft für Soziologie in Frankfurt 2010. CD-Rom. Wiesbaden 2012.

8 P. Eisewicht / M. Pfadenhauer, Freizeitliche Gesellungsgebilde? – Subkulturen, Teilkulturen und Szenen, in: R. Frericks / D. Brinkmann (Hrsg.), Handbuch Freizeitsoziologie, Wiesbaden 2015, 489–512.

9 G. Betz / R. Hitzler / M. Pfadenhauer (Hrsg.), Urbane Events, Wiesbaden 2011.

Vermarktungslogik propagieren, die auf Protest, Selbstverwaltung bis hin zu Subsistenzwirtschaft abheben. Selbst in ihren extremen Formen stehen sie strukturell in einem gleichsam ‚parasitären' Abhängigkeitsverhältnis zum gesellschaftlichen ‚Wirt' und dessen Infrastruktur- und Entsorgungsleistungen, weshalb sie weder als Exodus noch als Eskapismus angemessen beschrieben sind.[10] Öffentlichkeitswirksame Ausdrucksformen wie Urban bzw. Guerilla Gardening machen deutlich, dass hier im Unterschied zur Happening- und Bewegungskultur aus den 1970er Jahren der Spaßfaktor und Eventcharakter bedeutsam ist.[11] Selbst bei spiritualistischen Anleihen sind „graduelle Positionierungen, ein Sowohl-als-Auch",[12] d. h. Hybridität[13] das wesentliche Merkmal.

3. Kultisch vereint

Der Postmoderne-Theoretiker Michel Maffesoli bezeichnet den sich unter den skizzierten Individualisierungsbedingungen abzeichnenden Trend zu einem solchen Vergemeinschaftungsmodus als „Rückkehr der Stämme".[14] Derlei Vergleiche drohen zu mythologisieren, wenn sie nicht empirisch geerdet werden: Der erste Unterschied zwischen den *neuen* Stammeskulturen und ihren archaischen Vorgängern besteht darin, dass sie *keine* existentielle Bedeutung an sich haben, sondern lediglich imaginäre Gebilde derer sind, die sich – wie auch immer – auf sie beziehen. Zweitens sind diese neuen Stammeskulturen typischerweise auch nicht verortbar in speziellen, eingrenzbaren Territorien. Drittens sind Clans und Pozzes in diesen Stämmen nicht organisatorisch, sondern eher kultisch vereint. Viertens sind sich nicht auf Dauer gestellt, sondern basieren eher auf einem

10 Vgl. in diesem Sinne Bernhard Kohl und Thomas Eggensperger in diesem Band, 31–39.

11 G. Betz, Vergnügter Protest. Erkundungen hybridisierter Formen kollektiven Ungehorsams, Wiesbaden 2016, Zugleich: Dissertationsschrift.

12 Vgl. B. Kohl / Th. Eggensperger in diesem Band, 31–39.

13 M. Pfadenhauer, In-Between Spaces. Pluralism and Hybridity as Elements of a New Paradigm for Religion in the Modern Age, in: Human Studies, 39/1 (2016), 147–159.

14 M. Maffesoli, The Time of the Tribes: The Decline of Individualism in Mass Societies. London 1996.

wackeligen Balance-Akt vielfältiger Eigenheiten und Sonderintressen von Cliquen und lokalen Gruppierungen. Und fünftens sind sie eher im Außen- als im Innenverhältnis aufeinander verpflichtet.

Der archaisierende Terminus „Stamm" ist also zwar reizvoll, aber selbst in der Konkretion „neo-tribe" irreführend. Gemeint ist eine soziale Aggregation, die *nicht*-zweckrational organisiert, sondern *kultisch* fokussiert ist. Was unsere Klischees von Stammesgemeinschaften aufleben lässt ist das von Zygmunt Bauman beschriebene Phänomen, dass diese Aggregationen *„in den Augenblicken ihrer Verdichtung … eine buchstäblich atemberaubende Intensität erreichen"* können.[15] In diesen Momenten der Afferveszenz versichern sich die davon erfassten Personen – nicht nur mental, sondern leib-körperlich – der Existenz dieser Gemeinschaft und ihrer je eigenen Zugehörigkeit dazu.

Diese emotionale Hingabe ist der Schlüssel für das Verständnis *posttraditionale* Gemeinschaften. Denn sie sind eben nicht *mehr* als eine Idee, eine Imagination. Diese Art von Gemeinschaft existiert nur im *Glauben* an ihre Existenz; sie besitzt nur Autorität, weil ihr und solange ihr Autorität *zugestanden* wird. Das bedeutet nicht, dass sie nicht mächtig wäre. Aber die Macht dieser Gemeinschaften gründet nicht auf Zwang und Verpflichtung, sondern auf *Verführung*. Damit ist nun nicht Demargurgie konnotiert, sondern auf der einen Seite die bereits erwähnte häufig ökonomisch motivierte Bereitstellung von Rahmenbedingungen, der auf der anderen Seite die ungenierte Bereitschaft zur Inanspruchnahme dieser Produktionsleistungen und der (freie) Wille zur emotionalen Bindung an die Gemeinschaft korrespondiert. Diese Freiwilligkeit zeigt sich daran, dass die affektuelle Zugehörigkeit prinzipiell unbeständig und typischerweise auch eher kurzlebig ist.

Ein letzter wichtiger Unterschied zwischen diesen Neo-Tribes und ihrem archaischen Modell besteht in deren thematischer Fokussierung und ihrem teilzeitlichen Charakter. Diese posttraditionalen Gemeinschaften bedienen eines unter vielen Interessensgebieten, weshalb das Gemeinschaftsmitglied typischerweise *nicht* in der Totalität einer Stammeskultur aufgeht, sondern sich (eher über kurz als über lang) als Mitglied verschiedener, zum Teil konkurrierender,

15 Z. Bauman, Ansichten der Postmoderne, Hamburg/Berlin 1995, 20.

grundsätzlich instabiler ‚Stämme' erlebt. Solidaritäten und Loyalitäten entstehen dementsprechend weniger aus existentiellen Notwendigkeiten heraus, denn aus – eher emotional als rational motivierten – situativen Entscheidungen dafür, (wiederum situativ) prosozial zu (inter-)agieren. Die relativ schwach ausgeprägte Arbeitsteilung unter den Mitgliedern der neuen Stämme führt dementsprechend symptomatischerweise auch nicht zu dem, was Emile Durkheim (1988) „organische Solidarität" genannt hat – also zu einem hochgradigen und nahezu alternativlosen, existentiellen Angewiesensein des einen Mitglieds auf das andere bzw. auf dessen Leistungen und Produkte.

Zugehörigkeit zu einer posttraditionalen Gemeinschaft meint also nicht vordringlich Mit-Arbeiten, Sich-Einsetzen usw., sondern vor allem die Übernahme von Zeichen und Symbolen und den Vollzug von Ritualen, die für diese (Teilzeit-)Kultur symptomatisch sind, zu denen man sich durchaus auch überschwänglich bekennt. Diese Mitgliedschaft beruht a) auf einer Entscheidung, die b) auch anders ausfallen könnte, also kontingent ist; und die c) weit weniger werthaltig denn ästhetisch motiviert ist. D. h.: wenn von einem Bekenntnis die Rede ist, dann gilt dieses nicht gemeinsamen Wertsetzungen, die Solidarität stiften, sondern einer Lebensstil-Ästhetik. Kurz: Vergemeinschaftung ist ‚heute' dadurch gekennzeichnet, dass sich Individuen kontingent dafür entscheiden, sich freiwillig und zeitweilig mehr oder weniger intensiv als mit anderen zusammengehörig zu betrachten, mit denen sie eine gemeinsame Interessenfokussierung haben bzw. vermuten.

Die emotionale Hingabe und das daraus erwachsende Zusammengehörigkeitsgefühl rechtfertigt es, von Vergemeinschaftung zu sprechen. Mit dem Attribut ‚posttraditional' ist zum einen die veränderte Haltung der Partizipanten, zum anderen das mangelnde Sanktionspotential der Gemeinschaftskollektivs angedeutet, auf die abschließend einzugehen ist – womit nochmals Gesellschaft in den Blick rückt, innerhalb der sich diese Form der Vergemeinschaftung vollzieht.

4. Vergemeinschaftung in Gesellschaft

Posttraditionale Vergemeinschaftungen konstituieren sich typischerweise also dadurch, dass individualisierte Akteure sich aufgrund kontingenter Entscheidung in soziale Agglomerationen und deren Geselligkeiten einbinden, die durch *distinktives* Wir-Bewusstsein stabilisiert sind. Diese Form der Vergemeinschaftung besteht folglich wesentlich aus der Konstruktion einer *gemeinsamen* ‚Außenseite'. D. h., das Verhältnis zu anderen konstituiert sich (auch) in dieser Gesellungsform im Akt der Vergemeinschaftung und in der Fortdauer der Gemeinschaft in Abgrenzung zu „Dritten" und in Ausgrenzung dieser „Dritten" aus der Wir-Beziehung.

Auch wenn solche Dritte manchmal in konkreter Form auftreten, ist für posttraditionale Gemeinschaften generell symptomatisch, dass dieser „Dritte" eher die Gesellschaft als solche ist, in der sich die Individuen vergemeinschaften: in diesem Fall wird die Gesellschaft symptomatischerweise erlebt als „Dickicht" relativ undurchschaubarer, ja teilweise unerklärlicher sozialer Umstände und Gegebenheiten. Denn das gesellschaftliche Erwartungsgeflecht scheint den Gesellschaftsmitgliedern vielerlei Verhaltensweisen aufzuerlegen und sie nicht nur in formalisierte Verkehrsregeln, sondern ungeschriebene Gesetze im Umgang mit anderen hineinzuzwingen, deren Einhaltung einem auferlegt erscheint, ohne dass Tradition (also ein ‚Es-gehört-sich-halt-so') als Instanz ausreichen würde. Und die gesellschaftliche Garantie deren Einhaltung durch die anderen Gesellschaftsmitglieder ist höchstens noch ein Versprechen, das zu häufig uneingehalten erscheint.

Aus der Komplexität der modernen Gesellschaftlichkeit erwachsen also vielfältige Defizite des generell postulierten Ordnungsanspruchs. Infolgedessen machen Individuen und Gruppierungen unausweichlich Erfahrungen nicht nur von Ungleichheit, sondern auch von Ungerechtigkeit, denn immer mehr soziale Ungleichheiten bzw. deren Konsequenzen werden als „ungerecht" empfunden (z. B. die Unterstützung von Flüchtlingen, aber auch eine als parasitär empfundene Kinderlosigkeit). Diese persistierende Idee von (Un-) Gerechtigkeit macht aus Ungleichheiten jederzeit entzündbare Konfliktstoffe und generalisiert die soziale Auseinandersetzung um Ressourcen und Lebenschancen. Das irritiert die kulturell geregelten

Gewohnheiten des Umgangs miteinander und bewirkt, dass tendenziell immer mehr Individuen und Gruppierungen die dergestalt tradierten gesellschaftlichen ‚Verkehrsformen' in Frage stellen.

Vor diesem Hintergrund verspricht die *posttraditionale* Gemeinschaft immerhin eine wenigstens *relative* Sicherheit und Fraglosigkeit im Hinblick auf die als gemeinsam veranschlagten Interessen. Allerdings resultiert aus der Dialektik von Integration und Distinktion unter Individualisierungsbedingungen eine strukturelle *Prekarität* dieser Vergemeinschaftungsform v. a. hinsichtlich der Frage, ob und inwieweit sich aus den konstitutiven Akten dieser Formen der *Ver*gemeinschaftung heraus überhaupt (relativ dauerhafte) *Gemeinschaften* entwickeln und stabilisieren (lassen). Denn um eine wechselseitige Verlässlichkeit zu sichern, müssten die als gemeinsam bzw. gemeinschaftlich *veranschlagten* Interessen auf Dauer gestellt, transformiert oder mythisiert werden. Erst dann wäre die Gemeinschaft als Gemeinschaft auch für den Fall garantiert, dass der (ursprüngliche) Anlass zur Vergemeinschaftung entfällt bzw. in Vergessenheit gerät.

Während traditionale Gemeinschaften nun typischerweise vielfältige solche kohäsionssichernde Sanktionspotentiale und Zwangsstrukturen aufweisen, die auf die Etablierung und Stabilisierung eines klar definierten und geregelten Innen-Außen-Verhältnisses abzielen, gilt dieses Prinzip in wesentlich geringerem Maße für die *posttraditionale* Form von Gemeinschaft: Denn in sie tritt der Einzelne nicht mehr (wie in einen Verein, eine Kirchengemeinde oder Partei ein, sondern er gruppiert sich typischerweise freiwillig, absichtlich und ohne viel Aufhebens dazu, und ebenso (relativ) problem- und folgenlos bleibt er dieser wieder fern.

Die sozialräumlichen Grenzen posttraditionaler Gemeinschaften verfließen folglich nach Innen ebenso wie nach Außen. (Nicht nur) deshalb können posttraditionale Gemeinschaften die Frage der Mitgliedschaft *nicht* wirksam sanktionieren. Sie können den Einzelnen zur Mitgliedschaft nicht verpflichten, sondern ihn in aller Regel lediglich zur Mitgliedschaft *‚verführen'*.[16] Diese ‚Verführung'

16 R. Hitzler, Verführung statt Verpflichtung. Die neuen Gemeinschaften der Existenzbastler, in: C. Honegger / S. Hradil / F. Traxler (Hrsg.), Grenzenlose Gesellschaft? Teil 1. Opladen 1999, 223–233.

geschieht wesentlich durch die Option zur Teilhabe an von den dadurch Angesprochenen als ‚erlebenswert' angesehenen sozialen Ereignissen. Derartige Ereignisse treten üblicherweise nicht zufällig ein, sondern sind in der Regel (kalkulierte) kollektive ‚Ausbrüche' aus der Banalität des Alltäglichen. Der bereits zitierte Gesellschaftstheoretiker Zygmunt Bauman konstatiert deshalb: „Sich dem Handeln anzuschließen, ist alles, was es zu teilen gibt. Was üblicherweise zu Zeiten des Karnevals als kurzer Bruch der Kontinuität, als fröhliche Aufhebung des Zweifels zum Vorschein kommt, wird nun zum Lebensmodus."[17]

Dies impliziert eine (so gut wie) „unheilbare" strukturelle Labilität der posttraditionalen Gemeinschaft: sie droht jederzeit zu verfallen, wenn sich niemand mehr findet, der sie ‚umtreiben' oder ihr angehören will. Deren sozialintegrative Wirkung ist für die an ihr Teilhabenden aber annäherungsweise mit der traditionellen Funktion eingelebter Milieus vergleichbar: Sie stellt ein einigermaßen plausibles Repertoire an Relevanzen, Regeln und Routinen zur Verfügung, das von den Mitgliedern zumindest in dem Maße, wie sie sich auf die Gemeinschaft beziehen und verlassen (wollen), mehr oder weniger akzeptiert und auch hinlänglich übernommen wird. D. h. (auch) die posttraditionale Gemeinschaft ist in all ihren Erscheinungsformen eine ‚Antwort' auf die allgemeine gesellschaftliche Verunsicherung.[18]

* * *

17 Z. Bauman, Ansichten der Postmoderne, Hamburg/Berlin 1995, 354.

18 R. Hitzler / A. Honer / M. Pfadenhauer, Posttraditionale Vergemeinschaftung: Eine ‚Antwort' auf die allgemeine gesellschaftliche Verunsicherung, in: K. Dörre / J. Lessenich (Hrsg.), Unsichere Zeiten. Verhandlungen des 34. Kongresses der Deutschen Gesellschaft für Soziologie in Jena 2008, Wiesbaden 2010, 371–382.

Summary: Michaela Pfadenhauer, Mechanisms of belonging in post-traditional communities

Michaela Pfadenhauer (Vienna | Austria) notes that although societies today can only be described in terms of processes, they are not without structure in this ongoing process of modernisation: new, post-traditional forms of socialisation are emerging. However, these new forms no longer drawn their community-building power from people's similar social circumstances, but rather from similar life goals and similar forms of aesthetic expression.

Pfadenhauer sees emotional commitment as the key to understanding post-traditional communities, which exist only because there is belief in their existence and which have authority only because and for as long as their authority is accepted.

In this context, types of post-traditional community formation still promise relative security and a relatively unquestioning acceptance of interests deemed as shared. However, there is another side to community development in the context of individualisation: the inherent contradiction between integration and distinction renders community development in this form structurally precarious, not least when we consider whether communities can in fact develop or stabilise reasonably sustainably in this way at all. Post-traditional communities are therefore to be considered fundamentally structurally instable: they can disintegrate at any moment as soon as people cease to wish to belong to them.

Ulrich Engel

Thesenpapier: Kirche

Eine Teilperspektive des Forschungsprojekts „Gemeinschaft und Individualisierung. Was hält Gesellschaft und Kirche zusammen?" (2014–2016) hatte sich zur Aufgabe gemacht, den systemischen Zustand der kirchlichen Kohäsionskräfte auf ihre Zukunftsfähigkeit hin zu untersuchen. Was, so die Leitfrage, hält Kirche hierzulande in ihren Inneren, d. h. in ihren konkreten Praxisgestalten einschließlich ihrer institutionellen Verfasstheit, zusammen? Reflektiert wurde die Frage vor dem Hintergrund dessen, was in grober Skizzierung als post/säkulare oder mundane[1] Gesellschaftsformation bezeichnet werden kann.[2]

1.

Über Jahrtausende hinweg stand Gott im Mittelpunkt der symbolischen Ordnung der Dinge.[3] Himmel und Erde, Ewigkeit und

1 Zum Begriff „mundan" im vorliegenden Zusammenhang vgl. Th. Eggensperger, Keine Angst vor der Welt. Individualisierung im Raum des Mundanen, in: εὐangel 3 (2013), http://www.euangel.de/ausgabe-3–2013/glauben-in-saekularitaet/keine-angst-vor-der-welt/ [Aufruf: 13.6.2016].

2 Vgl. dazu insgesamt die publizierten Ergebnisse des vorhergehenden Forschungsprojekts „Glaubensvermittlung in religiösen und gesellschaftlichen Transformationsprozessen": Th. Dienberg / Th. Eggensperger / U. Engel (Hrsg./Eds.), Woran glaubt Europa? Zwischen Säkularisierung und Rückkehr des Religiösen // What Does Europe Believe In? Between Secularization and the Return of Religious Life, Münster 2010; Th. Dienberg / Th. Eggensperger / U. Engel (Hrsg.), Säkulare Frömmigkeit. Theologische Beiträge zu Säkularisierung und Individualisierung, Münster 2013; Th. Dienberg / Th. Eggensperger / U. Engel (Hrsg./Eds.), Himmelwärts und weltgewandt. Kirche und Orden in (post-)säkularer Gesellschaft / Heavenward and Worldly. Church and Religious Orders in (Post) Secular Society, Münster 2014; M. N. Ebertz / L. Segler, Orden und Säkularisierung. Ergebnisse aus Befragungen von Mendikanten in Deutschland, Österreich und der Schweiz (Kultur und Religion in Europa Bd. 10), Berlin 2015.

Zeitlichkeit, Kirche und Saeculum strukturierten diese Ordnung, die spätestens mit der Aufklärung zusammengebrochen ist. War die symbolische Ordnung bis dahin „auf ein transzendentes ‚Du' ausgerichtet, welches mit dem Terminus ‚Himmel' auch eine Lokalisierung und ein Zentrum fand, so begann sie mit dem Verlust des göttlichen Palastes um eine Leere zu kreisen, die alle Sinnpotentiale zu verschlingen droht."[4] Die nun leer gewordene Mitte hat dem Abendland massive Traumata beschert. Friedrich Nietzsche (Stichwort: Tod Gottes[5]) und Michel Foucault (Stichwort: Tod des Subjekts[6]) haben den skizzierten Verlust zum Ausgangspunkt ihres Denkens überhaupt gemacht.

These 1: *Eine theologische Reflexion über die Gemeinschaft der Kirche hat ihren Ausgangspunkt in der grundstürzenden Demontage der symbolischen Ordnung einschließlich der damit einhergehenden institutionellen Erschütterungen der hierarchisch strukturierten ekklesía zu nehmen.*

2.

Im Philipperhymnus (Phil 2,6–8) wird die κένωσις, d.i. die Selbsterniedrigung Gottes im Christus Jesus, als Verzicht auf die ursprüngliche Gottesgestalt (v. 6a: „μορφῇ θεοῦ") einschließlich deren „Macht

3 Zum Folgenden s. U. Engel, Kirche unter leerem Himmel. Skizzen zu einer kenotischen Ekklesiologie für post/moderne Zeiten, in: www.futur2.org. Zeitschrift für Strategie & Entwicklung in Kirche und Gesellschaft 2/2015, http://www.futur2.org/article/kirche-unter-leerem-himmel/ [Aufruf: 13.6.2016].

4 K. Appel, Vom Preis des Gebetes, in: ders. (Hrsg.), Preis der Sterblichkeit. Christentum und neuer Humanismus (Quaestiones disputatae Bd. 271), Freiburg/Br. 2015,186–228, hier 187.

5 Vgl. F. Nietzsche, Die fröhliche Wissenschaft, in: ders., Sämtliche Werke. Kritische Studienausgabe in 15 Bänden, G. Colli / M. Montinari (Hrsg.), München Neuausgabe 1999, Bd. 3, 343–651, hier 480–482.

6 Vgl. M. Foucault, Die Geburt einer Welt. Aus dem Französischen übersetzt von M. Bischoff, in: ders., Schriften in vier Bänden. Dits et Ecrits. Bd. I 1954–1969, hrsg. von D. Defert / F. Ewald unter Mitarbeit von J. Lagrange, Frankfurt/M. ^{3}2014, 999–1003, hier 1002.

und Herrlichkeit"[7] bekannt; am Ende des kenotischen Prozesses verbirgt sich Christus in der Gestalt eines Sklaven (v. 7b: „μορφὴν δούλου"). Eduard Schweizer hat darauf aufmerksam gemacht, dass es hier gerade nicht bloß um einen Wandel der äußeren Erscheinungsform geht, sondern dass Phil 2 direkt auf „den ‚Status', die Position, die Stellung"[8] zielt. Im weiteren Textverlauf verbindet Paulus die göttliche Selbstentäußerung mit ethischen Mahnungen an die Gemeinde.[9] Damit überführt er die *kenotisch dekonstruierte Christologie* in eine gleichermaßen *kenotisch dekonstruierte Ekklesiologie*, deren Diskurs auf jedwede Repräsentation der göttlichen *potestas* im Modus einer *Ecclesia triumphans* verzichtet. Diese in Phil 2 mitgedachte kenotische Ekklesiologie spiegelt die reale Existenz einer einflusslosen Diasporagemeinde wider. Die Mitglieder dieser entäußerten *ekklesía* wissen um den eigenen Machtverlust und um das Prekäre ihrer Position; darin sind sie vielen „Menschen gleich" (Phil 2,7).[10]

Der Turiner Philosoph Gianni Vattimo (* 1936) vertritt in diesem Zusammenhang die These, dass alle heute zu beobachtenden Säkularisierungstendenzen in der christlichen Religion selbst angelegt sind: „Säkularisierung als positive Gegebenheit heißt, dass die Auflösung der sakralen Strukturen der christlichen Gesellschaft [...] nicht als Schwinden oder Verabschiedung des Christentums zu verstehen ist, sondern als eine vollkommene Erfüllung seiner Wahrheit, die [...] die kenosis ist, die Herablassung Gottes."[11]

7 O. Hofius, Der Christushymnus 2,6–11. Untersuchungen zu Gestalt und Aussage eines urchristlichen Psalms (*Wissenschaftliche Untersuchungen* zum Neuen Testament Bd. 17), Göttingen ²1991, bes. 57.

8 E. Schweizer, Erniedrigung und Erhöhung bei Jesus und seinen Nachfolgern, Zürich 1955, 54.

9 Hierzu und zum Folgenden vgl. R. Kampling, Das Lied vom Weg Jesu, des Herrn. Eine Annäherung an Phil 2,6–11, in: Bibel und Kirche 64 (2009), 18–22.

10 Zu den politischen Implikationen des Philipperbriefes insgesamt vgl. A. Zanotelli, Il Dio che si svuota. Filippesi: una comunità alternativa all'Imperio (Cammini dello Spirito vol. 5), Bologna 2014.

11 G. Vattimo, Glauben – Philosophieren. Aus dem Italienischen von Ch. Schultz, Stuttgart 1997, 44f.; vgl. dazu auch ders., Christentum im Zeitalter der Interpretation. Aus dem Italienischen von M. Weiß, in: ders. / R. Schröder / U. Engel, Christentum im Zeitalter der Interpretation, hrsg. von Thomas Eggensperger im Auftrag des Institut M.-Dominique Chenu – Espaces Berlin (Passagen Forum), Wien 2004, 17–32.

These 2: *Gemäß Vattimos These vom ‚schwachen Denken' („pensiero debole"*[12]*) ist ekklesiale Existenz in einer säkular gewordenen Gesellschaft systematisch-theologisch vornehmlich als ‚schwache' Existenz zu fassen. Zusammen mit Schweizers Analyse, nach der es Phil 2,6f. vor allem um die Dekonstruktion von Status, Position und Stellung zu tun ist, kann die schwache Kirche als eine ekklesía ohne Privilegien definiert werden – um Papst Franziskus zu bemühen: als „‚verbeulte' Kirche"*[13].

3.

Eine „verbeulte" Kirche ohne Privilegien ist in Identität und Handeln der gläubigen *Individuen* wie auch der *Gemeinschaft* als ganzer gekennzeichnet durch:

- das Schwinden des ehemals eindeutigen Duals „Mitgliedschaft" versus „Nicht-Mitgliedschaft". An dessen Stelle treten Phänomene eines sog. *Multiple Religious Belonging* (MRB). Entsprechende Entwicklungen in den Niederlanden zeigen dies deutlich. Vor diesem Hintergrund ist die Konstruktion ein neuen ekklesialen „Wir" nur als prozessual offen angelegte, individuell verantwortete Suchbewegung zu denken[14];
- das Schwinden traditioneller Institutionen gemeinschaftlichen Engagements, die vor allem auf verbindliche und dauerhafte Zugehörigkeit angelegt waren. An ihre Stelle treten – vornehmlich im urbanen Raum – zunehmend andersartig strukturierte *posttraditionale Vergemeinschaftungsformen*, die auf zeitlich begrenzte Engagements in inhaltlich

12 Vgl. ders. / P. A. Rovatti (Ed.), Il pensiero debole, Milano 1983.

13 Papst Franziskus, Apostolisches Schreiben „Evangelii Gaudium" über die Verkündigung des Evangeliums in der Welt von heute (Verlautbarungen des Apostolischen Stuhls Bd. 194), Bonn 2013, Nr. 49.

14 Vgl. M. Kalsky, Auf der Suche nach einem neuen „Wir", in: Junge Kirche 1 (2014), 32–38; R. Bernhardt / P. Schmidt-Leukel (Hrsg.), Multiple religiöse Identität. Aus verschiedenen religiösen Traditionen schöpfen (Beträge zu einer Theologie der Religionen Bd. 5), Zürich 2008.

klar umrissenen Projekten setzen. Vor allem die Verschiebung der Deutungs- und Entscheidungshoheit von der Institution hin zum Individuum zeichnet kommunitäre Engagements heute aus.[15] Entsprechende Entwicklungen sind im zivilgesellschaftlichen Stadtraum zu besichtigen: Barcamps, Guerillagärten und Tauschläden…[16]

These 3: *Eine zukünftige kirchliche Gestalt pastoralen Handelns (in urbe) hat diesen Entwicklungen im Blick auf die einzelnen Gläubigen/Suchenden wie auch im Blick auf gemeinschaftliche Engagements Rechnung zu tragen, indem sie:*

a| *pluralitätsfähig* wird und sich nicht vor Hybridformen des individuellen und des kommunitären Glaubensvollzugs fürchtet[17];

b| sich umorientiert von der traditionellen kirchlichen Sozialformorientierung hin zu einer *situativ-pastoralen Aufgabenorientierung*[18];

c| die neutestamentliche Kategorie einer *„(uneigentlichen) JüngerInnenschaft"* (d. s. neugierige AnhängerInnen, geheime JüngerInnen, Menschen, die zeitweise mit Jesus ziehen) theologisch rekonstruiert, da dieses Modell in besonderer Weise individualitätskompatibel, auf Begegnungserfahrungen aufbaut, subjektiv verantwortete Entscheidungen ernstnimmt[19];

15 Vgl. R. Hitzler / A. Honer / M. Pfadenhauer (Hrsg.), Posttraditionale Gemeinschaften. Theoretische und ethnografische Erkundungen (Erlebniswelten Bd. 14), Wiesbaden 2008.

16 Vgl. H. Rauterberg, Wir sind die Stadt! Urbanes Leben in der Digitalmoderne, Berlin 2013.

17 Vgl. J. de J. Legorreta Zepeda, Desafíos del pluralismo a la unidad y catholicidad de la iglesia. VI Simposio International de Teología, Santa Fé (México) 2002; ders., Hacia otros modelos de comunidad cristiana. Ser y hacer comunidad en sociedades en cambio, Santa Fé (México) 2015.

18 Vgl. R. Bucher, …wenn nichts bleibt, wie es war. Zur prekären Zukunft der katholischen Kirche, Würzburg [2]2012.

19 Vgl. G. Lohfink, Braucht Gott die Kirche? Zur Theologie des Volkes Gottes, Freiburg/Br. 1998, 205–216; s. auch die Weiterentwicklung durch Ulrich Engel in zwei Vorträgen im Rahmen des Forschungsprojekts: „Amt – JüngerInnenschaft – Volk. Biblische und systematisch-theologische Spotlights zu drei neutestamentlich überlieferten Vergemeinschaftungsformen einschließlich

d| innovativ-kreative Foren und *Anders-Orte*[20] für Suchende schafft, vor allem für jene, die in den bestehenden kirchlichen Strukturen keine Heimat gefunden haben – kurz: Vergemeinschaftungsmöglichkeiten für spätmoderne Stadt-Menschen. Dazu bedarf es subsidiärer kirchlich-institutioneller Rahmenbedingungen, um *Experimente* zu ermöglichen.[21]

e| Voraussetzung für eine solche experimentell-zukunftsoffene Kirchenentwicklung ist eine kommunitäre *Kultur, die auch Scheitern* einkalkuliert.

ihrer möglichen Relevanz für die Ordensausbildung" (Köln, Workshop mit Ausbildungsleiter*innen OFM, OFMCap, OP, 30.9.2015) und „Neue Gemeinschaftsformen im urbanen Raum. Ekklesiologische Konsequenzen" (Berlin, Fachtagung in Kooperation mit dem Bereich Pastoral im Sekretariat der DBK, 10.3.2016).

20 Vgl. M. Foucault, Andere Räume. Aus dem Französischen von W. Seitter, in: ders., Botschaften der Macht. Der Foucault-Reader Diskurs und Medien, hrsg. von J. Engelmann, Stuttgart 1999, 145–157.

21 Vgl. bspw. die Gemeinde „Zeitfenster" in Aachen, http://www.zeitfenster-aachen.de/ [Aufruf: 15.6.2016].

Ulrich Engel

Research Paper: Church

A partial position of the research project: "Community and Individualization. What links society and the Church?" (2014–2016) pursued the goal of examining the systemic condition of the ecclesiastical forces of cohesion and their survival in the future. The guiding question was: What keeps the church together in this society, i.e. in its concrete practical realization, its institutional composition included? This question was reflected upon on the background of what roughly could be sketched as the post-secular or mundane[1] formation of society.[2]

1.

Throughout the millennia, not just in the European dominion, God was in the center of the symbolic Order of Things.[3] Heaven and Earth,

1 To clarify the term "mundane" in this context cf. Th. Eggensperger, Keine Angst vor der Welt. Individualisierung im Raum des Mundanen, in: εὐangel 3/2013 http://www.euangel.de/ausgabe-3–2013/glauben-in-saekularitaet/keine-angst-vor-der-welt/ [Accessed: 06/13/2016].

2 Cf. the published findings of the previous research project: "Transference of faith in religious and societal transformation processes". Th. Dienberg / Th. Eggensperger / U. Engel (Hrsg./Eds.), Woran glaubt Europa? Zwischen Säkularisierung und Rückkehr des Religiösen / What Does Europe Believe In? Between Secularization and the Return of Religious Life, Münster 2010; Th. Dienberg / Th. Eggensperger / U. Engel (Hrsg.), Säkulare Frömmigkeit. Theologische Beiträge zu Säkularisierung und Individualisierung, Münster 2013; Th. Dienberg / Th. Eggensperger / U. Engel (Hrsg./Eds.) Himmelwärts und weltgewandt. Kirche und Orden in (post-)säkularer Gesellschaft / Heavenward and Worldly. Church and Religious Orders in (Post)Secular Society, Münster 2014; M. N. Ebertz / L. Segler, Orden und Säkularisierung. Ergebnisse aus Befragungen von Mendikanten in Deutschland, Österreich und der Schweiz (Kultur und Religion in Europa. Bd. 10), Berlin 2015.

Eternity and Timeliness, the Church and the Secular structured this Order of Things that collapsed with the Age of Enlightenment latest. Up until then the symbolic Order was aimed at "a transcendental 'Thou' which, by using the term 'Heaven', also had a locus and a center. With the loss of the heavenly palace, it started orbiting the void that threatened to devour all potentiality for meaning"[4] This voided center caused severe traumata in the Occident. Friedrich Nietzsche (Topic: Death of God[5]) and Michel Foucault (Topic: Death of Subject[6]) took this very loss as the point of departure of their thinking.

Statement 1: *Any theological reflection on the community of the church has to take its departure point from the foundation-shattering undoing of the symbolic order, including the subsequent institutional shattering of the hierarchically structured ekklesia.*

2.

In the hymn in the epistle to the Philippians (Phil 2:6–8), the κένωσις the Self-abasement of God in Jesus Christ is confessed as a renouncing of the original Gestalt of God (vs. 6a: "μορφῇ θεοῦ") including its "power and glory"[7]; at the end of the kenotic process, Christ is hidden in the Gestalt of a slave (vs. 7b: "μορφὴν δούλου"). Eduard Schweizer

3 For the following cf. U. Engel, Kirche unter leerem Himmel. Skizzen zu einer kenotischen Ekklesiologie für post/moderne Zeiten [Church under empty skies. Sketches towards a kenotic ecclesiology), in: www.futur2.com. Zeitschrift für Strategie & Entwicklung in Kirche und Gesellschaft 2(2015) http://www.futur2.org/article/kirche-unter-leerem-himmel/ [Accessed: 06/13/2016].

4 K. Appel, Vom Preis des Gebetes [The Cost of Praying], in: K. Appel (Hrsg.), Preis der Sterblichkeit. Christentum und neuer Humanismus [The Cost of Mortality. Christianity and new Humanism.] (Quaestiones Disputatae Bd. 271), Freiburg/Br. 2015, 186–228, here: 187.

5 Cf. F. Nietzsche, The Gay Science. With a Prelude in Rhymes and an Appendix of Songs. Ed. and transl. by H.W. Kaufmann, New York 1974.

6 Cf. M. Foucault, La Naissance d'un monde. Entretien avec J.-M. Palmier, Le Monde, supplément: Le Monde des Livres, no 7558, 3 mai 1969, p. VIII. – Dits Ecrits tome 1, Texte 68.

7 Cf. O. Hofius, Der Christushymnus Philipper 2,6–11. Untersuchungen zu Gestalt und Aussage eines urchristlichen Psalms (Wissenschaftliche Untersuchungen zum Neuen Testament Bd. 17), Göttingen [2]1991.

pointed out that in this case it is not so much a change with regards to the outer appearance but that Phil 2 rather aims at "the 'status', the position, the rank".[8] Later in this passage, Paul connects the divine self-effacement with ethical admonitions for the congregation[9]. This way he translates the *kenotically deconstructed Christology* in a similar *kenotically deconstructed Ekklesiology*, whose discourse renounces any representation of the divine *potestas* as the result of a realization of an *Ecclesia Thriumphans.* The proof that this kenotic Ekklesiology was intended can be found in the mirroring of an inconsequential diaspora congregation. The members of this self-abased *ekklesía* acknowledge their loss of power and the precariousness of their position; in that they are equal to "all human beings" (cf. Phil 2:7).[10]

Turin Philosopher Gianni Vattimo (*1936) formulated the statement that all tendencies for secularization that can be observed today within Christian Religion are self-authored. "Secularization as a positive given means that the disconnect of sacral structures of Christian society … is not to be understood as vanishing or departure of Christianity but as a completion of its truth, that is kenosis, the self-abasement of God."[11]

Statement 2: *In accordance with Vattimo's concept of 'weak thinking' ("pensiero debole"[12]), ecclesial existence in a secularized society is to be understood in systematic theological thinking as 'weak existence'. Together with Schweizer's analysis, according to which Phil 2:6 mainly attempts to define the deconstruction of status, position and rank, the weak*

8 E. Schweizer, Erniedrigung und Erhöhung bei Jesus und seinen Nachfolgern, Zürich 1955, 54.

9 Cf. for this and the following R. Kampling, Das Lied vom Weg Jesu, des Herrn. Eine Annäherung an Phil 2,6–11, in: Bibel und Kirche 64 (2009), 18–22.

10 With regards to the political implications of the Epistle to the Philippians cf. A. Zantonelle, Il Dio che si vuota. Filippesi: una comunità alternative all'impero (Cammini dello Spirito vol. 5), Bologna 2014.

11 G. Vattimo, Glauben – Philosophieren. Aus dem Italienischen von Christiane Schulz, Stuttgart 1997, 44f. Cf. also Id., Christentum im Zeitalter der Interpretation. Aus dem Italienischen von M. Weiß, in: R. Vattimo / R. Schröder / U. Engel, Christentum im Zeitalter der Interpretation, ed. by Th. Eggensperger on behalf of the Institut M.-Dominique Chenu – Espaced Berlin (Passagen Forum), Wien 2004, 17–32.

12 Cf. id. / P. A. Rovatti (eds.), Il pensiero debole, Milano 1983.

> *Church is to be understood as an ekklesía that owns no privileges, but has to establish authority [lat. "auctoritas"] solely by the power of convincing through her reasoning and her actions.*

3.

In identity and actions of her faithful individuals as well as the congregations as such, a "dented" Church without privileges is marked by:

- vanishing of a once clear dualism of "membership" vs. "non-membership". In its place there are *Multiple Religious Belonging* (such as in the Netherlands), respectively – in a broader sense – *Multiple Social Belonging*. The construction of a new ecclesiastical "we" has to be thought of as a searching movement that is conceived as an open process in individual responsibility[13];
- vanishing of traditional institutions of communal engagements that were based on commitment and long duration of belonging. In their place are – mainly in urban areas – increasingly differently structured post-traditional forms of establishing community that rely on time restricted engagements within well defined purposeful projects. More than anything, the shift of the authority of finding meaning and decision making from the institution to the individual marks today's communitarian engagements within the political, social and religious realm.[14] According developments can be found in the urban environment of civil society: Barcamps, Guerilla gardens, swap meets…[15]

13 Cf. M. Kalsky, Auf der Suche nach einem neuen "Wir", in: Junge Kirche 1 (2014), 32–38; R. Bernhardt / P. Schmidt-Leukel (Hrsg.), Multiple religiöse Identität. Aus verschiedenen religiösen Traditionen schöpfen (Beiträge zu einer Theologie der Religionen Bd. 5), Zürich 2008.

14 Cf. R. Hitzler / A. Honer / M. Pfadenhauer (Hrsg.), Posttraditionale Gemeinschaften. Theoretische und ethnographische Erkundungen (Erlebniswelten Bd. 14), Wiesbaden 2008.

Statement 3: *A future ecclesiastical Gestalt of ministry (in urbe) has to acknowledge and address these developments with regards to the individual faithful / those who are seeking as well as with regards to communal engagement by:*

a| *becoming able to support* pluralism, *and not be afraid of hybrid forms of communal expressions of faith;*[16]

b| *re-orienting herself from a traditionally ecclesiastical form (e.g. territorial Parishes) to a form that acknowledges the* situational, pastoral purpose orientation[17] *(e.g. congregation of individuals).*

c| *reconstructing theologically the category of an* "(in-essential) discipleship" *of the New Testament (i.e. curious adherent, clandestine disciple, people who for a time with follow Jesus on his way) because this model is extremely apt to take seriously individuals, experiences of encounter, and shared responsibility decisions*[18]*;*

d| *creating innovative and creative locals and Other-Spaces*[19] *for those who are searching, especially for those who are unable to find a home in existing church structures; for short: opportunities for community for the post-modern denizens of the urban area. This requires subsidiary conditions provided by church and institution*

15 Cf. H. Rauterberg, Wir sind die Stadt! Urbanes Leben in der Digitalmoderne, Berlin 2013.

16 Cf. J. de J. Legorreta Zepeda, Desafíos del pluralismo a la unidad y catolicidad de la iglesia. VI Simposio International de Teología, Santa Fé (México) 2002; Id. Hacia otros modelos de comunidad en sociedades en cambio, Santa Fé (México) 2015.

17 Cf. R. Bucher, … wenn nichts bleibt, wie es war. Zur prekären Zukunft der katholischen Kirche, Würzburg ²2012.

18 Cf. G. Lohfink, Braucht Gott die Kirche? Zur Theologie des Volkes Gottes, Freiburg/Br. 1998, 205–216. Cf. also its elaboration by U. Engel in two presentations within the research project: "Amt – JüngerInnenschaft – Volk. Biblische und systematisch-theologische Spotlights zu drei neutestamentlich überlieferten Vergemeinschaftungsformen einschließlich ihrer möglichen Relevanz für die Ordensausbildung" (Köln, Workshop mit Ausbildungsleiter*innen OFM, OFMCap, OP, 30.9.2015) und „Neue Gemeinschaftsformen in urbanen Raum. Ekklesiologische Konsequenzen" (Berlin, Fachtagung in Kooperation mit dem Bereich Pastoral im Sekretariat der DBK, 10.3.2016).

19 Cf. M. Foucault, Of Other Spaces: Utopia and Hererotopias. Translated by J. Miskoviec, in: Architecture, Movement, Continuité 5 (1984), 46–49.

to allow and experiments *and facilitate their* continuation *once they have been evaluated positively.*[20]

e| *Creates conditions for such an experimental and open-to-the-future development of the Church, which is a communitarian culture that acknowledges failure ("trial and error").*

20 Cf. for example the Congregation "Zeitfenster" [Time-Window] in Aachen, http://www.zeitfenster-aachen.de [Accessed: 07/14/2016].

Manuela Kalsky

Ein neues Wir und die Kirchen

Meine Wahlheimat sind die Niederlande. Geboren und aufgewachsen in Deutschland, teile ich inzwischen die Realität vieler Migranten und Migrantinnen in Amsterdam: ich bin bikulturell. Seit 2011 gehört die Hauptstadt der Niederlande offiziell zu den superdiversen Städten dieser Welt. Sie ist eine sogenannte *majority-minority city*.[1] Das heißt: in Amsterdam gibt es keine ethnische Gruppe mehr, die die Mehrheit formt. 49 % der Einwohner Amsterdams sind Alteingesessene und 51 % haben einen Migrationshintergrund. 180 unterschiedliche Nationalitäten sind in der Stadt zu finden. Unausweichlich stellt sich die Frage: wo hinein soll man dann eigentlich integrieren?[2] Die Situation in Amsterdam ist keine Ausnahme. Auch andere europäische Städte werden im Zuge zunehmender Globalisierung und Migration multiethnisch. Inzwischen sind auch Rotterdam und Brüssel superdivers und in Kürze wird auch Antwerpen dieses Prädikat bekommen.

Migration verändert unsere Gesellschaften, stellt uns vor neue Herausforderungen. Das Leben wird komplexer und dadurch auch komplizierter. Unterschiedliche Sprachen, unterschiedliche kulturelle Gebräuche und religiöse Überzeugungen sind Teil des Alltags in den Großstädten. Pluralität ist nicht nur bereichernd, sie bringt auch Probleme mit sich. Die Angst vor dem Verlust national und kulturell geformter Identitäts- und Deutungsmuster beunruhigt zurzeit viele Bürger in Europa und schürt Gegensätze. Die drohende Gefahr terroristischer Anschläge, wie die in Brüssel, Paris und Berlin, begangen von IS nahen jungen radikalisierten Moslimen, die

1 S. Vertovec, Super-diversity and its implications, in: Ethnic and Racial Studies, 30 (2007) 6, 1024–1054.

2 M. Crul, e.a, Superdiversiteit. Een nieuwe visie op integratie, Amsterdam 2013; D. Geldof, Superdiversiteit. Hoe migratie onze samenleving verandert, Leuven/Den Haag [4]2014.

oftmals in den jeweiligen europäischen Ländern aufgewachsen sind, führt zu Misstrauen und Spannungen innerhalb der Gesellschaft. Wir-Sie-Denken floriert und wird politisch von nationalistischen Kräften genutzt. Auch in den als tolerant zu Buche stehenden Niederlanden ist das seit dem Mord an dem Cineasten Theo van Gogh in 2004 der Fall. Die islamfeindliche und anti-europäische Partei der Freiheit von Geert Wilders fand stets mehr Anhänger und wird laut Umfragen bei der Parlamentswahl im März 2017 in den Niederlanden die zweitgrößte Partei.

Die Scheinwerfer der niederländischen Medien richten sich nach dem Motto: ‚nur schlechte Neuigkeiten sind Neuigkeiten', in erster Linie auf Gewalttaten und kriminelle Vergehen, die von Migranten verübt werden. Eine der Folgen dieses Vorgehens ist das verzerrte Bild der gesellschaftlichen Wirklichkeit. Ein Beispiel: Eine Dame meldet sich zu Wort bei einem meiner Vorträge über die veränderte religiöse Landschaft in den Niederlanden: „Sie sagen, dass 5–6 % unserer Bevölkerung Muslime sind. Das kann nicht stimmen. Sie haben, denke ich, verkehrte Zahlen." Ich reagiere, dass ungefähr eine Million Muslime in den Niederlanden leben und frage sie, warum sie denkt, dass das nicht stimmt? „Es müssen viel mehr sein, sie stehen jeden Tag in der Zeitung", erwiderte sie.

Aus Untersuchungen geht hervor, dass in allen europäischen Ländern Menschen meinen, dass wesentlich mehr Muslime in ihrem Land leben, als tatsächlich der Fall ist. Diese Bildformung schürt Gefühle der Bedrohung hinsichtlich der Stellung der eigenen Gruppe: Angst vor dem Verlust von Arbeitsplätzen, von kulturellen Werten und den damit verbundenen Errungenschaften, die letztendlich auch das eigene Selbstbild in Frage stellen.[3] Die Abgrenzung der einen gegenüber der anderen Gruppe wird gefördert und der garstige Graben zwischen dem ‚Wir' und ‚die Anderen' vertieft sich. Islamfeindlichkeit beruht demnach nicht auf negativen persönlichen Erfahrungen mit Muslimen, sondern auf dem, was Sozialpsychologen als ‚Syndrom der gruppenbezogenen Menschenfeindlichkeit' bezeichnen. Bei diesem Syndrom handelt es sich um 'eine generalisierte Abwertung von Fremdgruppen, die im Kern von einer Ideologie

3 Vgl. https://www.welt.de/gesundheit/psychologie/article125838872/Angst-schuert-Islamophobie-und-Fremdenfeindlichkeit.html [Aufruf: 12.04.2017].

der Ungleichwertigkeit bestimmt ist'.[4] Nicht nur Islamophobie fällt darunter, sondern auch Fremdenfeindlichkeit, Rassismus, Antisemitismus, Sexismus und Homophobie. Eine Ideologie der Ungleichheit speist unterschiedliche Vorurteile.[5]

Lautlose Revolution

Wer meint, dass die schnellen gesellschaftlichen Veränderungen in den Niederlanden und die daraus entstehenden Angstreaktionen ausschließlich durch Migration verursacht wurden, täuscht sich. Nicht nur von außen, sondern auch von innen hat sich eine nahezu lautlose Revolution im Land vollzogen. In weniger als einem Jahrhundert transformierte eine sehr christliche Nation in eines der meist säkularisierten Länder Europas. 2 % der NiederländerInnen war zu Beginn des 20. Jahrhunderts kein Mitglied einer Kirche, heute gibt 67,8 % der niederländischen Bevölkerung an, keine Bindung mehr zu einer Kirche zu haben.[6] Acht Jahre zuvor war das noch 60 %. In der neusten Untersuchung, die unter dem Titel *Gott in den Niederlanden* seit 1966 jede zehn Jahre durchgeführt wird, gab 24,5% der niederländischen Bevölkerung an, Mitglied einer Kirche zu sein. Davon gehörte 11,7% der katholischen Kirche an, wobei jedoch nur 1,2 % dieser Gläubigen am Sonntag den Gottesdienst besucht.[7] Von römisch-katholischer Seite wurde in 2016 offiziell bekannt gegeben, dass in den nächsten 15 Jahren voraussichtlich 1200 von den 1500 römisch-katholischen Kirchen ihre Türen schließen werden. Den protestantischen Kirchen ergeht es nicht viel besser. Bereits in 2013 wurde von kirchlicher Seite angekündigt, dass ungefähr die Hälfte der 2000 protestantischen Kirchen in

4 A. Zick / B. Küpper / A. Hövermann, Die Abwertung der Anderen. Eine europäische Zustandsbeschreibung zu Intoleranz, Vorurteilen und Diskriminierung, Forum Berlin, Friedrich Ebert Stiftung 2011, 43.

5 Ebd., 42–48, Abb.1, 44. Vgl. ebenfalls: A. Zick u. a. The syndrome of Group-focused Enmity. The interrelation of prejudices tested with multiple cross-sectional and panel data, in: Journal of Social Issues, 64 (2008) 2, 363–383.

6 T. Bernts / J. Berghuijs, God in Nederland 1966–2015, Utrecht 2016. Die nun folgenden Zahlen beziehen sich auf diese Studie.

7 8,6 % der niederländischen Bevölkerung ist Mitglied der Protestantischen Kirche der Niederlande (PKN) und 4,2 % rechnet sich zu den kleinen protestantischen Kirchen.

den kommenden Jahren überflüssig wird. Entweder bekommen diese Kirchen eine neue Bestimmung oder sie werden abgerissen.

Der Leerlauf der Kirchen in den Niederlanden, ist hinlänglich bekannt. Neu jedoch an der Untersuchung *Gott in den Niederlanden 2016* ist die Diversität an Glaubensüberzeugungen innerhalb der jeweiligen Kirchen. So hat von den 11,7% katholischen Gläubigen nur noch 17% eine theistisches Gottesvorstellung, 40% gehört zu den sogenannten ‚Ietsisten' (ich glaube an ‚Etwas'), 30% sind Agnosten und 7% gibt an Atheist zu sein. Eine interessante Mischung, die deutlich macht, wie sehr auch innerhalb der Kirchen – in diesem Fall der katholischen Kirche – eine Diversität an ‚Glaubensvorstellungen' zu finden ist. Auch im protestantischen Bereich ist diese Diversität sichtbar, auch wenn das theistische Gottesbild mit 34% etwas höher liegt und sich ‚nur' 3% der Befragten Atheist nennen. Fazit: Nicht nur außerhalb, sondern auch innerhalb der Kirchen ist eine große Diversität an Glaubensformen zu finden.

Post-christlich

Wohl kaum hätte jemand vor 70 Jahren gedacht, dass Christen in den Niederlanden anno 2016 eine Minderheit wären. Auch ist die Situation der etablierten Kirchen zweifellos dramatisch, es wäre falsch daraus den Schluss zu ziehen, dass es in einer post-christlichen Gesellschaft – was die Niederlande laut dieser Studie sind – kein Bedürfnis mehr nach Religion oder Religiosität gäbe. Immerhin bezeichnet sich die Mehrheit der NiederländerInnen noch immer als ‚gläubig' oder ‚spirituell'. Die religiös-lebensanschauliche Landschaft der Niederlande ist vielfältig geworden: Theisten, Ietsisten, Agnosten, Atheisten, Humanisten, Muslime, Hindus, Juden, Buddhisten, neue Spirituelle, etc. Sie alle haben unterschiedliche Vorstellungen von dem, was sie ‚unbedingt angeht' (Tillich), was sie im Leben aus spiritueller Sicht berührt und leitet. Woran man in den Niederlanden glaubt, ist nicht länger ein- sondern mehrdeutig. Ein beträchtlicher Teil der alteingesessenen NiederländerInnen sind ‚flexibele Gläubige' geworden, die nicht mehr in traditionell-religiöse Schubladen passen.[8]

8 M. Kalsky / F. Pruim, Flexibel geloven. Zingeving voorbij de grenzen van religies, Skandalon, Vught 2014.

Aus einer ebenfalls repräsentativen Umfrage, die 2014 unter der niederländischen Bevölkerung durchgeführt wurde, geht hervor, dass 23% der NiederländerInnen Elemente aus unterschiedlichen religiösen und lebensanschaulichen Traditionen kombiniert. Ein Phänomen, das im theologischen Bereich als *Multiple Religious Belonging* (MRB) angedeutet wird.[9] Hierbei geht es um Menschen, die Anhänger von zwei oder mehr religiösen Traditionen sind[10] oder Elemente aus unterschiedlichen Religionen und Weltanschauungen miteinander kombinieren. Während die *dual belonger* sich bewusst mit unterschiedlichen religiösen Traditionen und den dazugehörigen Gemeinschaften verbinden, betrachten die meisten MRB'ers religiöse und lebensanschauliche Traditionen als offenes Erbe, aus dem sie eklektisch schöpfen. Welche Rituale oder Weisheitstexte sie wählen, hängt von der Funktion ab, die sie in dem Moment in ihrem Leben spielen.

Der (post)moderne mündige (west-)europäische Mensch des 21. Jahrhunderts nimmt sich die Freiheit, Richtung und Werte im eigenen Leben selbst zu bestimmen, unter Zuhilfenahme einer Varietät an Lebensanschauungen und religiösen Ausdrucksformen, die ihm oder ihr im Freundeskreis, bei Kollegen, beim Reisen oder Surfen im World Wide Web begegnen. Religiöse Identität ist nicht länger an eine spezifische Religion gebunden. Sie ist veränderlich und vielfältig und lässt sich von unterschiedlichen religiösen Erfahrungen und Einsichten bereichern. Hier wird Vielfalt nicht als Bedrohung der eigenen Identität wahrgenommen, sondern als Bereicherung, ein Geschenk der Schöpfung. Eine nicht nur in den Niederlanden

9 Am Dominikanischen Studienzentrum für Theologie und Gesellschaft (DSTS) und an der Vrije Universiteit Amsterdam werden zur Zeit Forschungsprojekte zum Thema der multireligiösen durchgeführt, das die Hybridisierung der Religiosität in den Niederlanden untersucht. Die genannte Prozentzahl ist einer repräsentativen Umfrage dieses Forschungsprojekts entnommen. J. Berghuijs, Multiple Religious Belonging in the Netherlands. An Empirical Approach to Hybrid Religiosity, in: Open Theology 1 (2017) 3, 19–37. Vgl. zu diesem Thema auch: M. Kalsky ‚Religiöse Flexibilität. Eine Antwort auf kulturelle und religiöse Vielfalt, in: R. Bernhardt / P. Schmidt-Leukel (Hrsg.), Multiple religiöse Identität. Aus verschiedenen religiösen Traditionen schöpfen (Beträge zu einer Theologie der Religionen Bd. 5), Zürich 2008, 219–242.

10 R. Drew, Buddhist and Christian? Explortion of Dual Belonging, Routledge 2013.

wahrzunehmende Entwicklung.[11] An die Stelle eines soliden Glaubensfundaments von der Wiege bis zum Grab ist das Prinzip des *panta rei* getreten. Was gestern noch voll Überzeugung feststand, wird heute bereits wieder in Zweifel gezogen. Unterschiedliche lebensanschauliche Überzeugungen fließen ineinander und führen im kulturellen und religiösen Bereich zu hybriden Identitäten. Bei diesen ‚neuen Gläubigen' werden die Grenzen der eigenen religiösen Tradition fließend und zuvor voneinander geschiedene religiöse Welten miteinander verbunden. Der niederländische Soziologe Joep de Hart umschreibt diese Ausdrucksform von Religion als „dynamisch und offen, persönlich gefärbt und aktiv, nicht institutionell und pragmatisch".[12]

Von Einheit zur Vielfalt

Europa steht heute vor einem Paradigmenwechsel. Das Denken in Einheitskonstruktionen wird durch eine Denkweise der Vielfalt herausgefordert. Die nostalgischen Versuche eine langjährige europäische Kultur der Nationalstaaten, basierend auf der Einheit von Sprache, Territorium und Religion, neu zu erstellen, müssen durch ein Kulturkonzept ersetzt werden, das in der Lage ist, multiple Identitäten zu integrieren. Der Schlüssel für das, was im Leben und Glauben heute wichtig ist liegt in den Erfahrungen von Menschen, die in einer multiethnischen und multireligiösen Gesellschaft leben und überleben. Vielfalt erfordert Kommunikation. Das heißt, wir müssen den Dialog intensivieren und Verbundenheit fördern, wo wir einander meiden. Es gilt Antworten zu finden auf Probleme und Herausforderungen für die gemeinsame Zukunft, wie beispielsweise: Wie können wir eine friedliche und gerechte Gesellschaft schaffen, die es Menschen ermöglicht, in einem multiethnischen Europa zusammenzuleben? Wie können Vorurteile und Angst vor anderen Glaubensrichtungen abgebaut werden, ohne die Probleme zu verleugnen,

11 P. Zulehner, Spirituelle Dynamik in säkularen Kulturen? Deutschland – Österreich – Schweiz, in: Religionsmonitor 2008, Gütersloh 2008, 152–154; S. Huber, Analysen zur religiösen Praxis. Ein Blick in die Schweiz, in: ebd. 163.

12 J. de Hart, Zwevende gelovigen: Oude religie en nieuwe spiritualiteit, Amsterdam 2011.

die entstehen, wenn Menschen aus verschiedenen Kulturen und Religionen zusammenleben? Wie können wir uns und unserer Gesellschaft helfen, von den Früchten kultureller und religiöser Unterschiede zu profitieren, um das gute Leben für alle zu entwickeln?

Die Suche nach diesem ‚guten Lebens für alle' ist meines Erachtens die zeitgemäße Übersetzung dessen, was im christlichen Bereich mit dem Reich Gottes gemeint ist. Es geht darum ein vielfältig religiöses, spirituelles und humanistisches Publikum zur Zusammenarbeit einzuladen, um das zu tun, was im christlichen Glauben die Botschaft des Juden Jesu beinhaltet: Gerechtigkeit schaffen für die Schöpfung Gottes und sich mit Leidenschaft und Mitgefühl umeinander kümmern. Die Sehnsucht nach diesem neuen Wir, das sich nicht über Ausschluss der Anderen, sondern in Verbindung mit ihnen definiert, lädt alle ein sich am Bau des gemeinsamen Hauses zu beteiligen. Ein Haus, in dem Herkunft und unterschiedliche Lebensüberzeugungen nicht verleugnet, aber auch nicht überbewertet werden und wo beim Bau die Talente *aller* gefragt und eingesetzt werden. Kurz und gut: es geht darum eine Gesellschaft aufzubauen, in der sich alle zu Hause fühlen können, basierend auf gegenseitigem Vertrauen und individueller Verantwortlichkeit, genährt von lebensanschaulichen und religiösen Weisheitstraditionen.[13]

Projekt W!R

Der Wunsch beizutragen an einem derartigen ‚neuen Wir' hat die Arbeit am theologischen Forschungszentrum der niederländischen Dominikaner (DSTS) in den letzten acht Jahren bestimmt.[14] Es ist die Aufgabe des Studienzentrums, im Rahmen dominikanischer Spiritualität gesellschaftliche und religiöse Zukunft mitzugestalten, wobei die *circumspectio* – sich umschauen und wahrnehmen, was Menschen beschäftigt – deren Wichtigkeit bereits Thomas von Aquin betonte, als Ausgangspunkt dient. Anschluss suchen bei der Lebenspraxis der Menschen, ihren Ängsten und Sorgen, Freuden

13 J. Sacks, The home we build together. Recreating society, London 2007.

14 Mehr Information über das Dominikanische Studienzentrum für Theologie und Gesellschaft ist zu finden unter www.dsts.nl.

und Hoffnungen, ist dabei unerlässlich. Im Mittelalter standen die Dominikaner auf dem Marktplatz wo sich das alltägliche Leben abspielte. Heute ist dieser Marktplatz das Internet. Die Welt um uns herum versuchen zu begreifen und die Früchte davon mit anderen zu teilen – das *contemplari et contemplata aliis tradere* der dominikanischen Bruderschaft – betrachten wir als Auftrag des Studienzentrum und Fortsetzung der dominikanischen Tradition.

Eine Gruppe Wissenschaftler aus unterschiedlichen Fachbereichen arbeitete zur Frage, welche Voraussetzungen ein derartiges ‚neues Wir' braucht. Auch wurde mit Unterstützung des niederländischen Ministerium für Infrastruktur, Wonen und Milieu (VROM) die interreligiöse Dialogplattform Nieuwwij.nl ins Leben gerufen, um ein breites Publikum an dieser Suche zu beteiligen. Gemeinsam formten sie Projekt W!R, das sich zum Ziel gesetzt hat, den garstigen Graben zwischen ‚Wir' und ‚den Anderen' zu überbrücken. Um deutlich zu machen, dass es sich bei diesem Projekt nicht um die Stabilisierung des bereits vorhandenen ‚Wir' handelt, sondern um neue Gemeinschaftsformen, wurde für das Logo die Schreibweise W!R gewählt, wobei das Ausrufezeichen die Dringlichkeit dieses Unternehmens unterstreicht.

Nieuwwij.nl bietet *Infotainment* – eine Kombination von Information und Entertainment. Initiativen und Menschen sind in Videos auf der Website zu sehen, die sich für dieses neue Wir einsetzen: in Politik und Wissenschaft, in Kunst und Ökonomie, in den unterschiedlichen Religionen, aber auch in kleinen persönlichen Nachbarschaftsinitiativen, in denen Menschen kreativ und mit wenig Mitteln Verantwortung nehmen für die *civil society*. Was inspiriert sie? Welche Werte stehen im Vordergrund? Warum setzen sie sich hierfür ein?

Das Generation Y-team, das für den Inhalt der Site verantwortlich ist, sucht in Gesellschaft und Religion nach Antworten auf diese Fragen. In der Breite der inhaltlichen Beiträge spiegelt sich die multikulturelle und multireligiöse Zusammensetzung des Teams. Muslime, Hindus, Christen, Buddhisten, Atheisten, Spirituelle, Agnosten, Humanisten – sie alle äußern sich in Videos und Interviews zu diesen Themen. Bekannte NiederländerInnen schreiben Kolumnen, Artikel und Kommentare und alle Website-BesucherInnen sind eingeladen darauf zu reagieren und Ideen auszutauschen. Viele der

Beiträge werden von anderen Medien übernommen, wodurch ein breites Publikum erreicht wird. Eine Übersicht und Beschreibung der unterschiedlichen Gruppen, die sich in den Niederlanden mit dem interkulturellen und interreligiösen Dialog beschäftigen, gehört zum festen Service-Bestandteil der Website.[15]

Wer die Website in der Hoffnung besucht, dort ein fertiges Rezept für ein neues Wir zu finden, wird enttäuscht werden. Was dort wohl aber geboten wird, sind inspirierende Ideen, Gespräche, Informationen und Meinungen über die benötigten Zutaten. Worum es geht, ist Vertrauen schaffen durch Kommunikation: Austausch, Kontakt, einander kennen und verstehen lernen in der Überzeugung, dass damit auch gegenseitige Ängste und Vorurteile vermindert werden. Was kann uns helfen Verbindungen zu vertiefen, anstatt Zwiespalt und Vorurteile zu fördern? Wann fühlen wir uns ‚zu Hause' und welche Aspekte in den verschiedenen lebensanschaulichen Traditionen können uns helfen, das gute Leben für alle zu gestalten?

Inzwischen ist Nieuwwij.nl mit mehr als 80.000 Besuchern pro Monat die größte digitale Plattform auf dem Gebiet der interreligiösen und interlebensanschaulichen Kommunikation in den Niederlanden. Im Herbst 2016 haben sich vierzig professionelle Trainer bei Projekt W!R angeschlossen, die dazu ausgebildet werden in Schulen und anderen Bereichen der niederländischen Gesellschaft Trainingsprogramme anzubieten, die sich auf das Verbinden kultureller und lebensanschaulicher Unterschiede richtet und ein Denken in ‚sowohl … als auch' fördert.

Ohne bestreiten zu wollen, dass das Leben in diverser werdenden Gesellschaften Probleme mit sich bringt, liegt der Fokus von Projekt W!R darauf, positive Entwicklungen und Möglichkeiten aufzuzeigen, in der Überzeugung, dass Worte und Bilder nicht ‚unschuldig' sind. Sie reflektieren die Wirklichkeit nicht nur, sie kreieren sie auch. W!R will Menschen dazu motivieren, konstruktiv, kreativ und selbstbewusst an der Gestaltung des eigenen Lebens und der Gesellschaft mitzuwirken. Anstelle von Angst und Zynismus, will Projekt W!R die Entwicklung einer gemeinsamen

15 Ein englischer Trailer zum Projekt ist zu finden unter http://www.nieuwwij.nl/over-nieuwwij/.

Kultur fördern, in der Unterschiede fruchtbar gemacht werden und das Recht, ‚anders zu sein' als eine demokratische Errungenschaft umarmt wird. Der Streit um die Frage, welche Werte dabei relevant sind und welche Elemente aus den jeweiligen religiösen und nicht-religiös-humanistischen Lebensanschauungen in der Gesellschaft eine Rolle spielen sollen, ist Teil der öffentlichen Diskussion. Die Debatte hierüber sollte nicht als ein Problem, sondern als ein Privileg aufgefasst werden. In einer offenen Gesellschaft, die nach der Verwirklichung der Emanzipation des Einzelnen strebt, wird es immer Interessenkonflikte geben. Die Gemeinsamkeit ist, dass Menschen sich an die Regeln halten, die in der Verfassung festgelegt sind.

Gegenseitige Akzeptanz und Gleichberechtigung mit Beibehaltung und Achtung der Unterschiede, sind unverzichtbare Bestandteile für die Entwicklung neuer nachhaltiger Verbindungen. Hier liegt der Grund für das gewählte Motto: ‚W!R – verbindet die Unterschiede'. Es unterstreicht die Notwendigkeit bei der Suche nach dem, was uns verbindet, Unterschiede positiv zu werten und nicht vorschnell zugunsten (vermeintlicher) Gemeinsamkeiten herunterzuspielen. Vielmehr geht es darum Unterschiede fruchtbar zu machen, was eine offene Haltung erfordert und das exklusive ‚Entweder / oder' um ein ‚Sowohl als auch' erweitert.

Im Plural denken zu lernen und darauf zu vertrauen, dass dieser Prozess nicht Identitätsverlust, sondern Identitätsgewinn zur Folge hat, ist die große Herausforderung vor der ein divers gewordenes Europa heute steht. Es bedeutet, jenseits der nationalen und kulturell-religiösen Nabelschau, Türen und Fenster zu öffnen und die Werte der unterschiedlichen Lebensanschauungen für das guten Lebens *für alle* zu nutzen. Es würde bedeuten die eigene Identität nicht durch Abgrenzung gegenüber den Anderen zu definieren, sondern in Beziehung zu ihnen. Eine Identität in Begegnung, die sich in Freiheit bereichern lässt von der Vielfalt humaner und religiöser Erfahrungen und Einsichten, die alles kritisch untersucht und letztendlich nur das weiterträgt, was dem guten Leben aller dient.

Die Kirchen und das neue Wir

Als Teil der individualisierten und globalisierten Gesellschaft entkommen auch die Kirchen nicht der Aufgabe, sich mit den neuen Zeichen der Zeit auseinanderzusetzen. Auch sie sind herausgefordert Antworten auf den Umgang mit religiöser Diversität zu finden und sich am Bau eines neuen Wir zu beteiligen. Inwieweit kann eine am christlichen Glauben orientierte Gemeinschaft religiöse Vielfalt umarmen und welche praktischen Konsequenzen ergeben sich daraus für die Amtsträger, die Gemeindemitglieder und die kirchlichen Lehrmeinungen? Wie verhält sich der Wahrheitsanspruch des christlichen Glaubens zu denen der anderen Religionen? Ist das Gebot der Stunde, die Grenzen der eigenen christlichen Identität inmitten einer stets größer werdenden Vielfalt an Religionen und Lebensanschauungen stärker zu bewachen oder sollten sie geöffnet werden für andere religiöse und nichtreligiöse Lebensanschauungen, um sich von ihnen befragen und möglicherweise auch bereichern zu lassen?

Den Kirchen in den Niederlanden fallen die Antworten auf diese Fragen schwer. Zu groß ist die Angst vor dem Verlust überlieferter Glaubenssicherheiten und der Verwässerung christlicher Werte. Von einer *Liquid Church*[16], die wie Wasser flexibel, fluide und veränderlich ist, ist im institutionellen kirchlichen Bereich noch wenig zu spüren. Aber um ein neues Wir in einer pluralen Gesellschaft zu verwirklichen, sind auch im religiösen Bereich Flexibilität, Netzwerkstrukturen und Verbindungen zu Menschen mit anderen gläubigen und nicht-gläubigen Lebensüberzeugungen gefragt. Auch innerhalb der Kirchen leben Vorurteilen, beispielsweise gegenüber dem Islam, die durch Begegnungen aufgebrochen werden müssen, um neue Wege der Verbundenheit zu finden. Auch in den eigenen Reihen gilt es die ‚Ideologie der Ungleichwertigkeit' zu demaskieren und ihr entschieden entgegentreten. Nur gemeinsam kann das ‚Syndrom der gruppenbezogenen Menschenfeindlichkeit', das sich in Europa in unterschiedlichen Formen von Fremdenfeindlichkeit erneut offenbart, unschädlich gemacht werden.

16 P. Ward, Liquid Church, Eugene 2013.

Es ist zu hoffen, dass es den traditionellen Kirchen und Theologen auch gelingen wird, eine Beziehung zu den ‚flexiblen Gläubigen' aufzubauen, indem sie die tief in der westlichen theologischen Tradition verankerte Abkehr vom Synkretismus, dem Vermengen von religiösen Traditionen, zu überwinden wissen. Die Wiederentdeckung der religiösen Vielfalt der eigenen Tradition und die darin verborgene Wahrheit, die zwischen dem Schon-jetzt und dem Noch-nicht immer in Bewegung ist, jenseits der Grenzen feststehender Lehrmeinungen und Identitätszuschreibungen, wäre dabei sicherlich hilfreich.[17] Auch wenn alle Umkehr und Erneuerung bei mir selbst anfangen muss, wie Dietrich Bonhoeffer einmal sagte, entlässt dies die Kirchen nicht aus ihrer Verantwortung den Zeichen der Zeit gerecht zu werden nach dem Motto: *Ecclesia semper reformanda est* – die Kirche ist immer zu reformieren. Was für die Gesellschaft gilt, gilt auch für die Kirchen: solange sie religiöse Vielfalt als eine Bedrohung des eigenen Glaubens auffassen und mit dem Verlust christlicher Identität und christlicher Werte in Verband bringen, kann kein ‚neues Wir' entstehen.

Ein neues Wir fordert zum theologischen Besitzverzicht auf. Es impliziert ein Offenhalten wegen dem, das noch kommen kann. Es benötigt Raum für das Andere, das Unerwartete, für Verwunderung. Damit rückt der eschatologischen Vorbehalt des christlichen Glauben ins Blickfeld der Theologie: der leere Stuhl auf dem der Messias einst sitzen wird.[18] Der Erlöser der Welt, auf den die Juden noch stets warten und von dem die Christen hoffen und glauben, dass es Jesus Christus sein wird, der wiederkehrt. Wäre mit dieser christologischen Leere ein Raum geschaffen, in dem Platz ist für eine Vielfalt an religiösen Heilsvorstellungen, in denen sich die Vollheit des guten Lebens für alle entfalten kann? Läge hier die Möglichkeit

17 Vgl. R. Panikkar, On Christian Identity. Who is a Christian?, in: C. Cornille (Ed.), Many Mansions? Multiple Religious Belonging and Christian Identity, Maryknoll / New York 2002, 121–144. Panikkar selbst ist christlich-hinduistisch-buddhistisch.

18 U. Engel, Autogene Selbstklimatisierung vs. radikale Heterologie. Gemeinschaft und/oder Gesellschaft denken mit Hieronymus Bosch, Peter Sloterdijk und Michel de Certeau, in: Th. Dienberg / Th. Eggensperger / U. Engel (Hrsg.), Auf der Suche nach einem neuen Wir. Theologische Beiträge zu Gemeinschaft und Individualisierung, Münster 2016, 127–141, hier 140.

einer Begegnungsstätte mit den Geschichten von Menschen aus unterschiedlichen Kulturen und Religionen, die miteinander nach Antworten auf die Frage suchen, was Unheil und Heil heute für sie bedeuten. Ein derartig soteriologisch geprägtes Suchkonzept denkt religiöse Identität flexibel und beziehungshaft und Unterschiede wären bereichernd für die eigenen Erfahrungen, anstatt bedrohlich. Momente göttlicher Wahrheit werden nicht in von vornherein festgestellten Wahrheitsansprüchen der jeweiligen Religionen gesucht, sondern in der Interaktion, in der Begegnung mit Menschen mit anderen religiösen Erfahrungen.[19]

Wunschdenken? Gut möglich. Dennoch: Kirche und Theologie müssen im Umgang mit der heutigen kulturellen und religiösen Diversität aufpassen nicht selbst an dem ‚Syndrom der Gruppenbezogenen Menschenfeindlichkeit' zu erkranken, indem sie es als Instrument für die eigene Identitätsstiftung hantiert in Abgrenzung gegenüber ‚den Anderen', vor allem in Bezug auf den Islam. Im Zeitalter wachsender multireligiöser und multiethnischer Diversität und den Spannungen die sich daraus ergeben, ist nicht die Abgrenzung zu den Anderen das Gebot der Stunde, sondern die Verbindung zu den religiösen und spirituellen Fremden in unserer Mitte.

* * *

Summary: Manuela Kalsky, A new We and the churches

Manuela Kalsky (Amsterdam | Netherlands) begins her exploration of a new We by discussing the pluralisation in European communities caused by migration, with a particular focus on the Netherlands.

Such changes within society naturally also affect the churches and beliefs within a given church. A trend towards *multiple religious belonging* (MRB) can be observed here: religious and philosophical traditions are seen as a heritage to be drawn upon eclectically.

19 M. Kalsky, Wahrheit in Begegnung. Die Transformation christlicher Identität angesichts kultureller und religiöser Pluralität, in: Christian Identity I / Christliche Identität I, Forum Mission Bd. 2, Luzern 2006, 29–52. Dies, Christaphanien. Die Re-Vision der Christologie aus der Sicht von Frauen in unterschiedlichen Kulturen, Gütersloh 2000, 311ff.

Religious identity is thus diverse and subject to change; diversity is not perceived as a threat to individual identity but rather as an asset.

This poses the question of how societies can benefit from the fruits of cultural and religious differences to develop a "good life for all" – a question that is, of course, also fundamental for churches and religious communities. Kalsky cites the project "W!R" at the theological research centre of the Dutch Dominicans as an example of best practice. The project is helping to shape the social and religious future in the context of Dominican spirituality.

Ultimately, we need to learn to think in the plural and to trust in this process strengthening identity. Theologically, we must therefore relinquish our possessions if we are to engage with religious diversity and participate in the construction of a new We. This is the modern translation of what, in the Christian context, is meant by the Kingdom of God.

Stephan Winter

Kirche als ‚Resonanzraum' in der entfalteten Moderne?!

Ulrich Engel hat verschiedene Zugänge zu einem radikal kenotisch orientierten Kirchenverständnis skizziert. Ich stimme dem Ansatz insofern grundsätzlich zu, als die Kirche, die Gemeinschaft der Christusgläubigen, von ihrer ureigenen Sendung her nicht anders gedacht werden kann denn als Teilhaberin an der Kenosis des Gottessohnes Jesus von Nazareth. Ich möchte aber die Thesen in kritisch-konstruktiver Absicht einer Relecture unterziehen bzw. einzelne Aspekte anders zu justieren versuchen.

Zu These 1: Hinter der ersten These stehen weitreichende Voraussetzungen v. a. bezüglich der Reflexion auf Moderne, Modernität und Modernisierung. Bei einer Ausarbeitung müssten diese Voraussetzungen deutlich expliziert und ihre Annahme begründet werden. Um nur beispielhaft anzudeuten, was dabei mindestens zu klären wäre[1]: Natürlich bedeutet die Aufklärung, wie Engel mit Appel herausstellt, einen tiefgreifenden geistesgeschichtlichen Einschnitt – doch: Was genau meinen hier der Begriff „Aufklärung" und dann – von der Beantwortung dieser Frage wesentlich abhängig – Begriffe rund um „Moderne"? Mittlerweile, so scheint es mir jedenfalls, lässt sich die Einsicht gut begründen, dass jeder Ansatz, der Aufklärung und Moderne zuerst und einseitig als Resultat einer „Subtraktion von überkommenen metaphysischen und religiösen Auffassungen"[2]

1 Vgl. u. a. die Beiträge in O. J. Wiertz (Hrsg.), Katholische Kirche und Moderne (Frankfurter Theologische Studien Bd. 73), Münster 2015, darin bes. den einführenden Aufsatz des Herausgebers: Katholische Kirche und Moderne. Welche Moderne – welche Kirche?, a. a. O., 1–66.

2 So im Anschluss an Taylor: H. Steinfath, Subtraktionsgeschichten und Transzendenz. Zum Status der modernen moralischen Ordnung, in: M. Kühnlein / M. Lutz-Bachmann (Hrsg.), Unerfüllte Moderne?, 599–622, 599; die Einstufung

zu begreifen sucht, „erbärmlich unzulänglich" daher kommt – gleich, ob er nun von Verächtern oder Verfechtern der Moderne vertreten wird. Ein solcher Zugang vermag schon den völlig unterschiedlichen Entwicklungen von Religion und religiöser Praxis im Kontext der Modernisierung nicht gerecht zu werden. Ich modifiziere die These Engels von daher wie folgt:

These 1: *Jede theologische Reflexion über die Kirche hat ihre Sichtweise auf Aufklärung und Moderne zu explizieren und gegenüber anderen Zugängen abzugrenzen. In diesem Zusammenhang sind apodiktische, global formulierte Aussagen über* die *Beziehungen von (katholischer) Kirche und Moderne eher zu vermeiden:* „Stattdessen ist im Einzelnen zu fragen, welche Moderne in welchem Verhältnis zur (katholischen) Kirche steht – wobei gelegentlich genauso zu fragen ist, zu welcher (Ausprägung der) (katholischen) Kirche. [...] Eine simple umfassende Antwort auf die Frage nach dem Verhältnis zwischen katholischer Kirche und Moderne wird weder der Komplexität des fragilen Experiments der Moderne noch der spezifisch katholischen Bewegungsform der pilgernden Kirche gerecht."[3]

Zu These 2: Auch mit der Bezugnahme auf Vattimos Konzept des „schwachen Denken" übernimmt Engel begründungslogisch weitgehende Verpflichtungen. Darauf ist hier nicht im Einzelnen einzugehen, zumal Engel selber bereits eine ausführlichere Auseinandersetzung mit Vattimos Ansatz vorgelegt hat.[4] In unserem Rahmen nur so

als „erbärmlich unzulänglich" in C. Taylor, Ein säkulares Zeitalter (engl. Original: A secular Age, Harvard 2007), aus dem Englischen von J. Schulte, Frankfurt/M. 2009, 455. Vgl. auch ders., Das Unbehagen an der Moderne (engl. Original: The Malaise of Modernity, *House of Anansi* Pr.: 1991), Frankfurt/M. 1995, 18f.

3 O. J. Wiertz, Kirche, a. a. O., 58.

4 Vgl. U. Engel „Philosophie (im Licht) der Inkarnation. Zu Gianni Vattimos Religionsdiskurs im Zeitalter der Interpretation, in: G. Vattimo / R. Schröder / U. Engel, Christentum im Zeitalter der Interpretation, hrsg. von Th. Eggensperger im Auftrag des Instituts M.-Dominique Chenu – Espaces Berlin (Passagen Forum), Wien 2004, 41–78. Engel gelingt es in diesem Beitrag, Vattimos Ansatz aus Sicht christlicher Theologie einzuordnen und zu würdigen. Er stellt dabei

viel: Vattimo gehört zu den Philosophen der Gegenwart, die das hermeneutische Denken im Anschluss v.a. an Heidegger und Gadamer zu radikalisieren suchen. Auf dieser Spur nimmt er an, dass sich die neuzeitliche Hermeneutik letztlich noch einmal restlos geschichtlich verstehen muss: „Wenn die Feststellung, daß es keine Tatsachen, sondern nur Interpretationen gibt, ihrerseits auch eine Interpretation ist [...], dann kann diese nur als interessegeleitete Antwort auf eine bestimmte geschichtliche Situation verstanden werden – nicht als objektive Kenntnisnahme einer Tatsache, die ihr äußerlich bleibt, sondern ihrerseits als eine Tatsache, die konstituierend in ebenjene geschichtliche Situation eingeht, mit der sie korrespondiert, auf die sie antwortet. [...] Die Hermeneutik ist keine Philosophie, sondern Darlegung

u.a. zu Recht fest, dass Vattimo „den Prozess der in der *kenosis* gegründeten Säkularisierung nur unter Inkaufnahme einer Abwertung des Ersten/Alten Testaments (und damit der jüdischen Tradition) denken kann" (a.a.O., 67). Und: „Kritisch zu fragen bleibt auch, warum eine Philosophie (im Licht) der *kenosis* das Fleisch als materialen Text der Inkarnation – und daran anschließend: die Materialität der sakramentalen Vollzüge – aus seinem [sic!] Religions-Diskurs durchgehend ausblendet." (a.a.O., 68). – Ein Kernproblem, das ich allerdings auch bei Engel nicht hinreichend bearbeitet sehe, ist Vattimos positive Rezeption von Heideggers Relecture der abendländischen Geistesgeschichte als einer von „Onto-Theologie" negativ geprägten Geschichte der Gewalt. Gemäß dieser Rekonstruktion ist das Auftreten des – v.a. mit Nietzsche identifizierten – Nihilismus deshalb zu begrüßen, weil dadurch „jenes Denken, welches das Sein mit dem objektiv Gegebenen identifiziert, mit dem Ding, was ich vor mir habe und dem gegenüber ich nicht anders kann, als die Haltung der Kontemplation einzunehmen, des staunenden Schweigens usw." überwunden wird. Verabschiedet werde damit jene „Metaphysik der Objektivität", die „[ab]schließt mit einem Denken [...], das die Wahrheit des Seins mit der Berechenbarkeit, Meßbarkeit und endgültigen Manipulierbarkeit des Objekts von Wissenschaft und Technik gleichsetzt": „Diese Kritik der Metaphysik hat [...] in erster Linie nicht theoretische, sondern ethisch-politische Grundlagen: Es geht nicht darum, der Ansicht vom Sein als Objekt eine adäquatere und wahrere Konzeption entgegenzusetzen, die immer noch objektiv wäre, sondern darum, aus einem Denkhorizont herauszutreten, der sich letztendlich als der Freiheit und der Geschichtlichkeit des Existierens gegenüber feindselig erwiesen hat." (G. Vattimo, Glauben – Philosophieren. Aus dem Italienischen (Original: Credere di credere, Milano, 1996) übers. v. Ch. Schultz (RUB Bd. 9664), Stuttgart 1997, 21f). Vgl. zu den fragwürdigen Voraussetzungen dieses Gesamtbildes u.a. die kritischen Analysen in Th. Schärtl, Metaphysische Blockaden. Eine Auseinandersetzung mit den philosophischen Dogmen in der Sakramententheologie Louis-Marie Chauvets, in: M. Stuflesser (Hrsg.), Fundamentaltheologie des Sakramentalen. Eine Auseinandersetzung mit Louis-Marie Chauvets ›Symbol und Sakrament‹ (Theologie der Liturgie Bd. 9), Regensburg 2015, 49–79, bes. 51–65.

des geschichtlichen Daseins als solchen im Zeitalter des Endes der Metaphysik.“[5] Hermeneutik versteht sich also radikal auch selbst erst einmal nur als Interpretation: als (quasi-)philosophische Interpretation der Interpretations‚philosophie‘. Doch Vattimo sieht damit kein Endlosverfahren in Gang gesetzt. Vielmehr entdeckt er ein normatives und unhintergehbares Moment, das – als kriterieller Faktor – als Bedingung der Möglichkeit aller Hermeneutik zugrunde liegt, weil es selbst nicht aus den zu deutenden Zeichen zu gewinnen und damit nicht abermals begründungsbedürftig ist: die Caritas/Liebe. Hier setzt seine These an, dass zwischen radikal zu sich selbst gebrachter Hermeneutik und dem christlichen Basisgedanken der Inkarnation ein Zusammenhang der „Transkription“[6] oder „Verwandtschaft“[7] besteht: eine Strukturparallele zwischen der christlichen Botschaft und dem Gang philosophischen Denkens. Christliche Gott-Rede folge der Logik der Entäußerung und führe *darin* dennoch auf einen letzten Grund, der als unhintergehbare Bedingung der Möglichkeit des „pensiero debole“ fungiert: „Die Interpretation, die Jesus Christus von den Prophezeiungen des Alten Testaments gibt, ja: die Interpretation, die er selber *ist*, enthüllt deren wahren Sinn, der am Ende nur einer ist: die Liebe Gottes zu seinen Geschöpfen. Und dieser ‚letzte‘ Sinn ist eben dadurch, daß er die *caritas* ist, niemals der wahrhaft ‚letzte‘, hat nicht die Letztgültigkeit des metaphysischen Prinzips, über das man nicht hinausgeht und vor dem jedes Fragen aufhört.“[8]

So etabliert Vattimo, obzwar radikal-hermeneutisch denkend, quasi in paradoxer Weise ein unhintergehbares Prinzip, das die intendierte Pluralität von Sinnansprüchen erst ermöglicht: „Obwohl er jegliche metaphysische Letztbegründung ausdrücklich ablehnt, nimmt er die Caritas qua Seinlassen performativ als formale Bedingung der Möglichkeit aller Pluralität in Anspruch. Das Begründende

5 G. Vattimo, Das Zeitalter der Interpretation, in: R. Rorty / G. Vattimo, Die Zukunft der Religion, hrsg. von S. Zabala. Aus dem Amerik. übers. v. M. Adrian / N. Fröhder (Verlag der Weltreligionen Tb. 12.), Frankfurt/M. 2009, 62–66, 54.55 (ital. Original: Il futuro della religione, Milano 2004).

6 G. Vattimo, Glauben – Philosophieren, a. a. O., 30.

7 G. Vattimo, Jenseits des Christentums. Gibt es eine Welt ohne Gott? Aus dem Ital. (Dopo la cristianità. Per un cristianesimo non religioso, Milano 2002) von M. Pfeffer, (amerik. Original: After Christianity, New York 2002), München 2004, 37.

8 Vattimo, Glauben – Philosophieren, a. a. O., 69.

an sich besteht im Offenhalten des Interpretationsprozesses gegen jedwede inhaltlich geschlossene Letztheit, sofern Caritas nicht als Inhalt, sondern als Ethos begriffen wird. Und damit ist eine Idee von Universalität gewonnen, deren Spezifikum genau darin besteht, dem Differenten Raum zu geben."[9]

Im Ergebnis führt Vattimos Denkweg damit meines Erachtens – entgegen seiner erklärten Absicht – zu einer (sogar recht exponierten) Deutung der Wirklichkeit im Ganzen – und damit zu mehr als einer kategorialen Ontologie, auf den Punkt gebracht: zu einer der Sache nach metaphysischen Position.[10] Ich sehe in einem solchen Befund ein wichtiges Indiz dafür, dass „die Metaphysik tatsächlich nicht am Ende ist"[11]. Und tatsächlich „bleiben berechtigte Zweifel, ob mit einem [...] nachmetaphysischen Vernunftbegriff die Probleme der Moderne zu bewältigen sind"[12]. Meine Überzeugung, die ich hier allerdings nicht weiter explizieren, geschweige denn begründen kann, ist, dass „auch in der Moderne [...] kein Weg vorbei [führt] an einem metaphysischen Absoluten", und der christlich-theistische Glaube, für den die Inkarnation wesentlich ist, scheint – darin wiederum ist den Impulsen Vattimos (modifiziert) zu folgen! – ein durchaus „aussichtsreicher Kandidat für die überzeugendste metaphysische Deutung der Wirklichkeit"[13] zu sein. So hebt Vattimo hinsichtlich

9 K. Müller, Glauben – Fragen – Denken, Bd. II: Weisen der Weltbeziehung, Münster 2008, 185.

10 Inwiefern Vattimo dies selber sogar ohne nachhaltige Folgen für die Stringenz seiner Argumentation einräumen könnte – und dies hier und da in seinen Schriften meiner Ansicht nach auch andeutet, wenn er von Metaphysik (lediglich?) im Sinne Heideggers spricht, die er gemeinsam mit Heidegger ablehne –, ist hier nicht zu diskutieren. Vgl. auch die Schlusspassage des schon zitierten Aufsatzes von Ulrich Engel, wo es heißt: „Vattimos ‚schwaches Denken' ist meines Erachtens über weite Strecken mit den Traditionen und Überzeugungen des Christentums vereinbar. Eine (halb-)gläubige Weltanschauung, die auf die Menschwerdung Gottes in dieser Welt und in dieser Zeit vertraut, braucht keine Metaphysik im heideggerschen Sinn [(!)]. Eine schwache Ontologie, die uns Menschen zur *caritas* ermutigt und befähigt, uns selbst als existierend und also auch als sterblich zu erfahren, ist sehr viel." (Engel, U., Philosophie, a.a.O., 68f)

11 H.-L. Ollig, Quo vadis Metaphysik?, in: ThPh 86 (2011), 321–341, 330.

12 Ders., Der Streit um die Moderne. Positionen der deutschen Gegenwartsphilosophie, in: ThPh 86 (2011), 1–33, 32; dort das nächste Zitat auf 33.

13 O. J. Wiertz, „Es ist immer, überall und für jeden falsch, etwas aufgrund von ungenügenden Beweisen zu glauben". Das Verhältnis von Glaube und Vernunft

des „Christentum[s] als geschichtlicher Heilsbotschaft" immer wieder hervor: Es ist ein Ausweis von Vernunft zu denken, „daß unsere Existenz deshalb von Gott abhängt, weil wir hier und heute unsere Sprache nicht sprechen und unsere Geschichtlichkeit nicht leben können, ohne auf die Botschaft zu antworten, die uns die Bibel übermittelt"[14]: „Diejenigen, die Christus folgten, als er sich ihnen in Palästina zeigte, taten das nicht nur, weil sie die Wunder gesehen hatten, und vor allem die vielen, die in den Jahrhunderten danach kamen, sahen die Wunder nicht. Sie glaubten, wie wir auf italienisch [sic!] oder deutsch sagen, ‚aufs Wort', oder auch: *fides ex auditu* – sie glaubten, weil sie gehört hatten. Die Bindung an Jesu Lehre ergibt sich durch die Überzeugungskraft der Botschaft selbst: Wer glaubt, hat verstanden, gefühlt, intuitiv erfaßt, daß Jesu Wort ein ‚Wort des ewigen Lebens' ist"[15]. Entsprechende Erfahrungen der Wahrheit sind aus dieser Perspektive nicht möglich „ohne irgendeine Form der Teilnahme an einer Gemeinschaft" bzw. an Gemeinschaften, die „ohne irgendeine unüberwindbare ‚objektive' Grenze (wie der Rasse, der Sprache, der ‚natürlichen' Zugehörigkeit) zusammentreffen."[16] – Von daher die Modifikation der zweiten These von Ulrich Engel:

These 2*: *Auch in der Gegenwart gibt es Ansätze aufrichtiger Wahrheitssuche, die sich der ausdrücklichen Reflexion auf eine Deutung der Wirklichkeit im Ganzen nicht verschließen, wie wir sie doch in allem Denken und aller Praxis mehr oder weniger deutlich voraussetzen. Ekklesiale Existenz in heutiger Gesellschaft wäre von daher systematisch-theologisch u. a. so zu denken, dass sie sich vom gelebten Glauben an den biblisch bezeugten (allmächtigen, allwissenden, moralisch vollkommenen und liebenden) Gott her wahrhaftig und aufrichtig als Gesprächspartnerin bei der Suche nach Wahrheit (in allen Kulturen) einbringt. Dabei wird sie sich, je mehr sie mit ihrem eigenen Glauben an Jesus von Nazareth als die letztgültige Offenbarung eben jenes*

unter den Bedingungen der Moderne. In: ders., Kirche und Moderne, a. a. O., 189–258, 250. Vgl. diesen Aufsatz für eine Darstellung der religionsphilosophischen Großwetterlage aus analytisch geschärfter Perspektive.

14 G. Vattimo, Zeitalter, a. a. O., 65.

15 Ders., Zeitalter, a. a. O., 64.

16 Ders., Zeitalter, a. a. O., 62.

Gottes ernst macht, an Jesu Botschaft von Gottes schrankenloser Güte orientieren, die keine gesellschaftlichen oder religiösen Zuordnungen kennt, und sie wird sich ggf. mit Jesus gar der Gewalt ausliefern lassen müssen, die für den Erhalt gewohnter und liebgewordener Strukturen und Privilegien kämpft. Darin vollendet sich dann die Sendung Jesu und abgeleitet davon die der Kirche durch Gott sowie in eins damit der menschliche Gehorsam: „Wer dies versteht, weiß, daß damit alle todbringende Gewalt ihre Kraft verloren, sich wirklich ‚ausgetobt' hat; daß wir keinen Grund mehr zur Angst haben. Diese Evidenz macht eine neue Kreatur aus uns (vgl. 2 Kor 5,14–17), bleibt aber nur dadurch lebendig, daß wir sie in unserer Existenz bezeugen. Allein in solcher Überlieferung wird die durch Jesu Auslieferung gewonnene Befreiung von den Mächten des Todes weiterhin offenbar"[17]. *Und dann gilt, wenn man etwa dem Evangelisten Markus (in der Urfassung) folgt:* „Jeder, der sich in Kirche wohl etabliert weiß und seine Stellung zu kennen glaubt, bekommt aber einen scharfen Spiegel seiner eigenen Erbärmlichkeit vors Gesicht gehalten, einfach indem der Evangelist den Weg des als Sieger bekannten Christus noch einmal abschreitet, bis hin zum Kreuz."[18]

Zu These 3: Den Optionen, die Engel im Rahmen seiner dritten These für eine heutige bzw. zukunftsfähige Gestalt der Kirche entwirft, stimme ich ausdrücklich zu. Ich möchte lediglich einen weiteren Aspekt ergänzen[19]: Diese Optionen werden vom jeweiligen kulturellen

17 H. Verweyen, Gottes letztes Wort. Grundriß der Fundamentaltheologie, 3. vollständig überarb. Aufl. 2000, Regensburg [4]2002, 54; vgl. a. a. O., 51–54.

18 Ebd., 385; vgl. dort 385–391, und ferner dazu auch S. Winter, Gottes Heilsplan nach dem Markusevangelium, in: M. Stuflesser / S. Winter, Wo zwei oder drei in meinem Namen versammelt sind, da bin ich mitten unter ihnen. Was ist Liturgie? (Grundkurs Liturgie Bd. 1), Regensburg 2004, 35–53.

19 Vgl. zum Folgenden ausführlich: M. Rohner / S. Winter, (K)eine Chance auf Resonanz? Kulturhermeneutische Erwägungen zum Verhältnis von christlicher Glaubenspraxis und säkularer Lebenswelt, in: T. Kettmann / J. Wübbe (Hrsg.), ZeitGeist?! Heutige Lebenswelten als heilsame Provokation für Theologie und Kirche. Festgabe für Bischof Dr. Franz-Josef Bode zum 25. Jahrestag seiner Bischofsweihe, Regensburg 2016, 34–50, sowie weitere einzelne Beiträge im

Kontext her zu spezifizieren sein. Eine am Inkulturationsparadigma orientierte Theologie und Praxis der Kirche ist insofern eine notwendige Ausfaltung ihrer kenotischen Existenz. – *Gaudium et Spes* 1 führt in diesem Zusammenhang den Resonanzbegriff ein: „Freude und Hoffnung, Trauer und Angst der Menschen von heute, besonders der Armen und Bedrängten aller Art, sind auch Freude und Hoffnung, Trauer und Angst der Jünger Christi. Und es gibt nichts wahrhaft Menschliches, das nicht in ihren Herzen seinen Widerhall fände (*quod in corde eorum … resonet*); die Gemeinschaft der Kirche erfährt sich so „mit der Menschheit und ihrer Geschichte wirklich engstens verbunden (*intime coniunctam experitur)*" (GS 1). Wenn das „wahrhaft Menschliche" im Innersten der Glaubenden „Widerhall", genauer: „Resonanz" findet, kann die heutige Welt ihnen eben nicht äußerlich bleiben; die Rede ist von einem buchstäblich „intimen" Verhältnis. So geht es bei der vom Konzil inaugurierten „Verheutigung" des Glaubens gerade nicht um eine modische Angleichung an den stets ambivalenten Zeitgeist, sondern die Hinwendung zur gegenwärtigen Lebenswelt gehört aus *intrinsischen* Gründen zum Auftrag der Kirche. Besonders explizit wird dies auch in Art. 4, in dem die berühmte Wendung von den „Zeichen der Zeit" zu finden ist: Zur Erfüllung ihrer Sendung, die darin besteht, „unter Führung des Geistes, des Trösters, das Werk Christi selbst weiterzuführen, der in die Welt kam, um der Wahrheit Zeugnis zu geben; zu retten, nicht zu richten; zu dienen, nicht sich bedienen zu lassen" (GS, Nr 3), sei die Kirche verpflichtet, „nach den Zeichen der Zeit zu forschen und sie im Licht des Evangeliums zu deuten". Dies könne aber, so der Art. 4 weiter, nur in der Weise geschehen, dass die Kirche „in einer jeweils einer Generation angemessenen Weise auf die bleibenden Fragen der Menschen nach dem Sinn des gegenwärtigen und des zukünftigen Lebens und *nach dem Verhältnis beider* zueinander Antwort geben" (*kursive* Hervorhebung S. W.). Welt und Evangelium stehen sich demnach nicht einfach wie Interpretandum und Interpretament gegenüber. Sie erschließen sich wechselseitig als ‚Orte' der Gottesbegegnung in den dynamischen Konstellationen menschlicher Suchbewegungen nach gelingendem raum-zeitlichen („gegenwärtigen") wie

genannten Sammelband. Die dortigen Ausführungen nehmen u. a. Anstöße auf aus H. Rosa, Resonanz. Eine Soziologie der Weltbeziehung, Berlin 2016.

dieses übersteigendem („zukünftigen") Dasein. Deshalb gilt es, „die Welt, in der wir leben, ihre Erwartungen, Bestrebungen und ihren oft dramatischen Charakter zu erfassen und zu verstehen."

Gemäß diesem Konzept ist die jeweilige Kultur unvermeidlich ein zentraler *locus theologicus,* ja: die Gegenwart ist in ihrer Ambivalenz und „Fragwürdigkeit" ein genuiner Erkenntnisort, um neu hineingeführt zu werden in die Weite und Tiefe des Glaubens. Wer das nicht wahrzunehmen bereit oder in der Lage ist, vergibt fahrlässig die Chance auf (neue) Resonanz: die Chance nämlich, dass der Heilige Geist *in* der Zeit als verborgen wirksam erfahren werden kann. Denn wie anders sollte sonst eine „Unterscheidung der Geister" ebenso zeitdiagnostisch profund wie spirituell fundiert möglich sein, die die „Zeichen der Zeit" so zu deuten vermag, dass Kirche der pfingstlichen Spur des Konzils und damit ihrer eigenen Botschaft treu bleiben kann? – Auch in dieser Hinsicht dürfte *Papst Franziskus* mit seinem Apostolischen Schreiben *Evangelii gaudium* in der Spur des Konzils einen lehramtlich epochalen Markstein gesetzt haben, wenn er programmatisch festhält: „Die Gnade setzt die Kultur voraus, und die Gabe Gottes nimmt Gestalt an in der Kultur dessen, der sie empfängt."[20] Der dabei anklingende altehrwürdige scholastische Grundsatz *gratia supponit naturam* erhält so eine überraschende „kulturalistische" Wende bzw., vorsichtiger formuliert: Die entsprechende *kulturhermeneutische* Sensibilität und Differenzierungskunst wird zur notwendigen Voraussetzung für jene „Inkulturation", durch die die „Freude des Evangeliums" – sprich: „Gnade" als „Gabe Gottes" – bei Menschen hier und heute erst „anzukommen" vermag. Kultur – und damit konkret auch: die säkulare Lebenswelt – bleibt dem Geschehen entsprechender „Glaubenskommunikation" nicht äußerlich. Die Kirche steht, pointiert gesagt, der säkularen Moderne nie undialektisch „gegenüber", sie hat sich vielmehr in ihr selbst zu entdecken. In all der Widersprüchlichkeit, Ambivalenz und Fragilität, die christliche Glaubenspraxis und säkulare Lebenswelt *miteinander teilen*, eröffnet sich dann der Raum wechselseitiger Resonanz, in dem das Geschenk Gottes fruchtbar werden kann, auf dass diejenigen,

20 Papst Franziskus, Apostolisches Schreiben „Evangelii Gaudium" über die Verkündigung des Evangeliums in der Welt von heute (Verlautbarungen des Apostolischen Stuhls Bd. 194), Bonn 2013, Nr. 115.

die so den Glauben suchen, „für alle eine Quelle der Freude und Zuversicht"[21] werden können.

Was dann der Kirche heute am meisten fehlt, ist nicht zuletzt der „Mut zur gläubigen Zeitgenossenschaft" in diesem Sinne – ein Mut, der sich insbesondere an der „Schnittstelle von Kultur und Glauben" zu bewähren hat.[22] Deshalb tut uns wohl „auch theologisch mehr Kulturhermeneutik not ohne dabei der Versuchung rein kulturwissenschaftlich arbeiten zu wollen, zu erliegen"[23]. Eine solche Kulturhermeneutik ist aus zuinnerst *theologischen* Gründen notwendig; ihre konkrete Bewährungsprobe aber dürfte in der Herausforderung liegen, ein differenziertes Gespür für die spezifisch säkular-postsäkularen[24] Verfasstheiten der Gegenwartskultur herauszubilden – und dieses Gespür innerhalb der Glaubensgemeinschaft zu kultivieren. Wenn man der Kirche empfehlen wollte, wo sie zuerst bei sich Resonanzpotentiale entdecken könnte, die ja als solche eben nicht machbar sind, wären wohl *erstens* glaubwürdige Lebensformen der Spiritualität zu nennen und *zweitens* Praxen einer Solidarität gerade mit den in vielerlei Art Bedrängten.[25] Damit sind zentrale Koordinaten der Kirche als eines (geistlichen) Raumes benannt, in dem

21 Vgl. Hochgebet für besondere Anliegen „Gott führt die Kirche".

22 Vgl. S. Ch. Kessler, Das Priesterliche in der Kirche – ein Plädoyer, in: M. Kehl / S. Ch. Kessler, Priesterlich werden. Anspruch für Laien und Kleriker, Würzburg 2010, 11–50, 28.

23 S. Orth, Hebammendienste gefragt. Zum Verhältnis von Theologie und Spiritualität, in: V. Hoffmann / G. M. Kleemann / S. Orth (Hrsg.), Unter Hochspannung. Die Theologie und ihre Kontexte, Freiburg/Br. 2012, 171–183, 177.

24 Der Hilfsbegriff soll andeuten, dass theoretische Rekonstruktionen von Signaturen religiöser Weltdeutungen bzw. von deren Entwicklung in der (entfalteten) Moderne mittlerweile äußerst komplex sein müssen, um ihr Erklärungspotential nicht schon im Ansatz zu schwächen. Hilfreich scheint diesbezüglich meines Erachtens nach wie vor z. B. Taylors Vorschlag zu sein, drei Säkularisierungsbegriffe voneinander zu unterscheiden; vgl. dazu u. a. C. Taylor, Säkulares Zeitalter, a. a. O., 45f.61–71.236f. Die Kategorie des Postsäkularen geht hingegen auf Habermas zurück. Vgl. bes. die Einführung des Begriffs in J. Habermas, Glauben u. Wissen. Friedenspreisrede 2001, in: ders., Zeitdiagnosen. Zwölf Essays, Frankfurt/M. 2003, 249–262. Als *postsäkular* bezeichnet in diesem Zusammenhang Jürgen Habermas eine Gesellschaft, die im Rahmen ihrer liberalen Selbstdefinition die eigenen säkularistischen Vorurteile reflektiert.

25 Vgl. T. Halík, Nachtgedanken eines Beichtvaters. Glaube in Zeiten der Ungewissheit, Freiburg/Br. 2012, 189. – Für eine Darstellung der entsprechenden „Grundhaltungen" Vertrauen, Offenheit und Unterscheidung, die Kirche hier zu kultivieren hat, vgl. E. Kunz, „Verwurzelt und weit". Spirituelle Grundhaltungen

christlicher Glaube – in Gestalt vielfältiger Ekklesien[26] – resonanzproduktiv zu werden vermag.

* * *

Summary: Stephan Winter, The Church as an "echo chamber" in the modern era?!

Stephan Winter (Münster | Deutschland) works on the basis of a radical, kenotic-centred understanding of the church, a concept which he develops through three different theses.

Thesis 1: Any theological reflection on the church must detail its view of enlightenment and modernity. General, categorical statements on the relationships between the church and modernity should if possible be avoided, as they allow neither for the complexity of the experiment that is modernity nor for the church as a movement.

Thesis 2: Even in the present, there are efforts to engage in a genuine search for truth that is open to reflection on the interpretation of reality as a whole. Ecclesial existence in today's society should therefore be thought of thus in systematic, theological terms: rooted

der Kirche in einer immer mehr globalisierten Welt, in: O. J. Wiertz, Kirche, a. a. O., 403–417.

26 Den Begriff führt ein: P. Hundertmark, Gemeinden gründen! Skizzen für eine Selbstorganisation der Christgläubigen, Annweiler o. J. [2015]. Hundertmark plädiert dafür, alle Sozialformen gelebten Glaubens radikal als Vorkommnisse der kommunikativen Praxis von Getauften zu verstehen. „Ekklesien" in diesem Sinne „bestehen ausschließlich aus Interaktionen, aus Handlungen, Begegnungen, Beziehungen, geteilten Erinnerungen, aus Meinungsbildung und Gespräch. Ihre Communio entsteht je neu aus ihrer ‚Communicatio'. [...] Christinnen und Christen schließen sich in Ekklesien freiwillig und selbstorganisiert zusammen, um gemeinsam dem Glauben Gestalt zu geben, um Gott zu feiern und in die Gesellschaft hinein zu wirken. [...] Wir ‚ekklesieren' wir vergemeinden uns, wir leben Kirche – aktuell, konkret, punktuell, hier und jetzt, je neu." (a. a. O., 15). Dies bedeutet freilich nicht, dass in dieser Konzeption kein systematischer Ort für eine (klassisch gesprochen:) u. a. auch hierarchische) Binnendifferenzierung der einzelnen Ekklesien und deren notwendige Einbindung in die Kirche als ihrer Gesamtheit vorgesehen wäre (vgl. dazu bes. P. Hundertmark, Gemeinden, Kap. 9: Ekklesien und Kirche; Kap. 10: Die Handelnden Personen; Kap. 13: Dienste und Aufgaben). Darauf kann hier nicht weiter eingegangen werden.

in a lived-out faith in the God to Whom the Bible bears witness, it genuinely and wholeheartedly commits itself as a partner for dialogue in the search for truth.

Thesis 3: A theology and practice oriented towards the paradigm of interculturation is a necessary expression of the church's kenotic existence. In this concept, the culture is inevitably a central locus theologicus. Church therefore needs credible forms of living spirituality and solidarity in practice to generate a genuine and productive resonance.

José de Jesús Legorreta Zepeda

The Identity of the Church

Amidst a plural and globalized modern world, "identity" is no longer a relatively homogeneous, static and essential reality. Rather, identity has become a problem, namely a heterogeneous, dynamic and precarious reality lacking both a fixed social nucleus and also an exclusive, immutable symbolic universe with general validity. In this new context, Berger and Luckman claim:

> *Unquestioned, secure knowledge dissolves into a no longer very compelling aggregate of loosely connected opinions. Firm interpretations of reality become hypotheses. Convictions become matters of taste. Commandments become suggestions.*[1]

In such circumstances, the preeminence of the individual and subjectivity have narrowed the capacity and operability of various institutions to their minimum (especially, religious institutions), with regard to their role as meaning-givers and thus as the institutions that were once self-understood as those who warranted or sanctioned identity. On the other hand, in this context institutions have been forced to "compete" with other similar institutions to secure "customers" who intend to shape, preserve and change their identity, but who also find themselves in front of a variety of possibilities to choose between without being constrained, though, to decide on one of them in particular[2]. Amongst the multiple consequences that derive from this last, institutions find it difficult to keep their traditions, beliefs, values, symbols and doctrines unchanged.

1 P. Berger / Th. Luckmann, Modernity, Pluralism and the Crisis of Meaning. The Orientation of Modern Man, Gütersloh 1995, 45–50.
2 The market analogy that underlies this statement has been masterfully explored by P. Berger, in: For a Sociological Theory of Religion, Barcelona 1981, chapter six.

As an institution situated in "today's world", the Roman Catholic Church has not remained exempt from such conditions proper to late modernity. This is despite the various efforts by important sectors of the Roman Catholic Church to preserve a stable and essential identity, endowed with coherence and unity, through a strengthening of authority and doctrinal discipline. Certainly, the attempt to delimit and safeguard ecclesial identity has been a permanent task of the church since its very beginnings, whether by recognizing and setting a "canon" of apostolic writings (the New Testament), by having a distinct ministerial structure (episcopes, priests, and deacons) or by instituting "margins" to interpret all the above (dogmas), among other concerns. Nonetheless, the modern sociocultural context has given rise to countless challenges to the identity of the church which cannot be confronted as in the past. For instance, although it is true that a gap has always existed between the ecclesial self-image of ordinary people (more symbolic and affective) and that of theologians and those who belong to the hierarchies (more conceptual and rational), today such a gap has not only been broadened but has entered–willingly or not– into the vertiginous vortex of modern pluralism, which inevitably produces a quasi-generalized situation of crisis.

This last has been aggravated by internal and external ecclesial factors such as,

a| the actual persistence of certain structures and mentalities in the church (proper to the Christendom era) that appeal to *authority* and to a supposedly ahistorical *tradition*, whose immutability and universality are considered as the first and last guarantors of "truth", contrary to the modern state of consciousness which requires justification for whatever is recognized as valid, just as it entails a processual, contextual and partial concept of "truth";

b| the loss of meaning of a large number of cultural expressions of faith identified with the pre-modern Mediterranean

c| The production of "communicative distortion" by the appearance of a religious and cosmovisional pluralism, in addition to its inherent conflicts of "translation" and articulation;

d| the reliance between every global proposal of meaning and individual sovereignty with its need of choosing freely;

e| and finally, we could mention the accelerated, syncretic and unequal social distribution of knowledge. These few but relevant elements tell us about a socio-historical conjuncture of social and thus ecclesial change that makes the crisis of identity, to which we have referred above, explicable.

At this point, it is necessary to contrast some empirical data with the theoretical approach to the identity of the church we mentioned, to either verify or challenge our hypotheses. There is no doubt that this task is immense since the identity phenomenon particularly that of the church is noticeably complex and multidimensional. Being conscious of the magnitude of this task, the present research intends to simply contribute to the continuation of the the discussion on ecclesial identity through an empirical study whose aims are: to identify some perceptions that Catholics (pointedly, lay Catholics) have about their church; to contrast these perceptions with the more elaborated views by theologians and the ecclesiastical hierarchy; and lastly, to explain the results in the frame of the modern plural context.

Therefore, this study is a "pilot experiment". With it, we expect to identify the degree of coherence that exists between the "idea" or the "image" of the church that the laity has, in relation to how ecclesial identity is articulated in some theological texts coming from the hierarchy and from academic theological discussion.

Regarding the first contrasting element that is required in this study (i.e. lay Catholics), the population universe must comprise at least three features: first, individuals must confess themselves as Catholics; second, they need to be settled within a sociocultural context that can be acknowledged as modern; third, it should constitute a universe sufficiently wide and plural so that its dominant features and tendencies can be expressed beyond some ethnic particularisms.

One of the universes that to a high degree meet the proposed requisites for this "pilot experiment" are the inhabitants of Mexico City, more specifically of Distrito Federal (DF). We must not lose sight that the opinions of the laity are not easily obtained. Namely, while we can easily get to know the opinion of the hierarchy and that of theologians through their published writings, the opinion of the laity is a matter whose examination and systematization is still pending nevertheless the many indirect assumptions that could be obtained in their concern. Hence there is the need to carry out an approach to the opinion of the laity through surveys.

With reference to the second contrasting element (i.e. official and specialized theological formulations about the identity of the church) we have chosen the "Dogmatic Constitution on the Church" (lg) of the Second Vatican Council and the "Catechism of the Catholic Church" (cat) published in 1992. Certainly, these are not texts at the same theological or literary level, nor the same level of authority (the Council is here preeminent). They do not strictly share equal aims either. What is more, these texts do not even keep total coherence with each other, which introduces the impossibility to see them as homologues in doctrinal terms. Nonetheless, in practice, both texts have turned into two of the great official referents that disclose the self-concept of church that the ecclesiastical hierarchy customarily holds. While *Lumen Gentium* mirrors the consensus of the episcopate worldwide, the *Catechism* illustrates– to a great degree– the interpretation and position that the Roman curia has with reference to conciliar ecclesiology. It is clear that in order to make this research manageable our choice implies a dismissal of many other official writings coming from episcopal conferences, dioceses, and even advisory bodies of the Holy See or documents written by the Pope himself.

As for the theological texts about the church, the challenge to dismiss some authors and opt for others is not an easy task. There is an extensive ecclesiological bibliography dispersed not only in diverse linguistic groups but mainly in different theological tendencies and approaches. Obviously, no choice would ever be fully representative of the wide range of stances and emphases that are today available in theological discussion. Despite the above, we need to decide on a source that meets some minimum criteria, namely: that it be a catholic theologian, whose ecclesiological thought can be situated in the great guidelines drawn by the Second Vatican Council, and whose theological position maintain a critical dialogue with modernity. From the wide range of authors that could have been considered under these criteria, we have opted for Medard Kehl and Juan Antonio Estrada.

Kehl's ecclesiology was principally elaborated in his work "The Church: Catholic Ecclesiology" (1992), once named "the best catholic

treatise at the present time"[3]. Here Kehl suggests a phenomenological method as a comprehensive approach and pays serious attention to the modern and global setting while maintaining his views within the lines of the ecclesiological horizon and church renovation that the Second Vatican Council proposed. On its side, Estrada's work essentially offers a polemical ecclesiology that criticises the endurance of the Christendom ecclesial model in today's institutions and church praxis. Furthermore, his work advocates church renovation by reassessing the laity also in the framework of Second Vatican Council's reports. Estrada's ecclesiology has been reflected, primarily, in three of his works: "The Church: Institution or Charism?" (1984), "The Church: Change and Identity" (1985), and "From the Mystery of the Church to the People of God" (1988)[4].
(...)

The Establishment of the Church

The debate raised within the Church about its origin, based on the results of historical-critical studies, has evolved into two approaches since the end of the nineteenth century: one that functions with a static, essential and ahistorical mentality and another that works with historical-critical categories[5]. Each of these mentalities has delineated ways to read and interpret the Scriptures and Tradition and, more concretely, the origin of church institutions. Hence, the first approach usually argues:

> *that the historical Jesus founded the Church by giving her a hierarchical governance structure through the election of the "twelve apostles" having Peter as the head. Accordingly, this institutional structure (endured in the episcopal collegiate presided over by the Pope) is normative for the organization of the Church of all times.*

3 C. O'Donnell / S. Pié-Ninot, „Kehl, Medard", in: Diccionario de Eclesiología, Madrid 2001, 615.

4 The original titles in Spanish are, J. A. Estrada, La Iglesia: ¿institución o carisma?, Salamanca 1984; La iglesia: identidad y cambio. El concepto de Iglesia del Vaticano I a nuestros dias, Madrid 1985; Del misterio de la Iglesia al Pueblo de Dios, Salamanca 1988.

5 J. A. Estrada, Para comprender cómo surgió la Iglesia, Estella 1999, 11.

On its side, the second approach would assert:

> *that Jesus' task and concern were how and when should the Kingdom of God be appointed, and not how to establish or organize a church (in an institutional sense). Therefore, if Jesus did not announce or organize the church, then he did not place Peter as its basis either. Accordingly, the organization of the church would be instead an ecclesial creation inspired by the Spirit and conditioned by the Jewish and Greco-Roman models of authority after the paschal experience.*[6]

From a diachronic perspective, it becomes problematic to outline an unequivocal association between one of this approaches and a certain group or subject (i. e. hierarchy or theologians) as in the last century we have witnessed a notable plurality of approaches in both groups. Nevertheless, it is possible to identify some tendencies. For instance, the statement of a historical establishment of the church by the historical Jesus has become to be a more or less constant approach in the ecclesiastical hierarchy, excepting the renovating statements of Vatican II. *Lumen Gentium* is very careful when it comes to exhibiting the origin of the church as a historical/salvific (theological) process. In this Constitution, the Council presents the Church as being primarily a "mystery" inserted in the salvific plan of the Trinitarian God (lg 1–4). From this perspective, the Council avoids pointing to a specific foundational "moment" of the church; it rather inclines to dynamic expressions that emphasize the origin of the church as a process, and whose immediate fundaments lay in the sayings and doings of the earthly Jesus, later continued in the reflection and practice of the apostolic communities under the Spirit's action.[7]

This mystical Trinitarian and historical-processual view on the origin of the Church that the Council proposed has not had a coherent reception in the official documents of the Magisterium. For example, while the *Catechism of the Catholic Church* (cat) embraces the conciliar proposal with regard to the origin of the Church

6 A detailed analysis from the exegetical point of view of the controversy between these two positions in relation to the origin of the church can be found in F. Schüssler Fiorenza, Foundational Theology, New York 1985; especially the second part entitled "The Foundation of the Church".

7 For example, LG 5 states that: "[…] The Lord Jesus set it on its course by preaching the Good News, that is, the coming of the Kingdom of God […]".

(cfr. 751–768), the text resulting from the "Third General Conference of the Latin American Episcopate" (1979), better known as *The Puebla Document* (DP), contends that:

> *The church is inseparable to Christ because He himself established it (cfr. LG 5b; 8c; GS 40b; UR 1a) by an expressed act of his will, on the twelve and whose head is Peter (cfr. Mt. 16,18) [...]. The church is not a late result, not a simple consequence unleashed by Jesus' evangelizing action. She is certainly born from this action but directly, for the Lord himself calls his disciples and partakes the power of his Spirit to them, endowing the nascent community with all the means and essential elements that the Catholic people profess as being a divine institution (DP 222. Our underlining).*

This text discloses that Jesus established the Church during his earthly life, with which the rejection to a processual understanding is emphasized. This idea that easily agrees with the ecclesiastical anti-modern statements at the end of the nineteenth century and beginnings of the twentieth[8], has been reproduced in catechisms. For instance, a catechism of the "Christian Doctrine" accepted by the Mexican Episcopate states:

> *Jesus Christ established the Kingdom and Family of God on Earth which is the Church, under the authority of the Pope and the other apostles. Jesus founded his church so that we could find divine life in her, the life He deserved for us with his death on the Cross.*[9]

The influence of such a statement on the great majority of Catholics in Distrito Federal has not been minor. When this population was asked about the origin of the church, 55 % agreed with the idea that "before his death and resurrection, Jesus Christ established a religious institution to which he called Church", whereas 45 % considered instead that "the church was born from a decision of the apostles

8 See, for instance, the "Oath Against Modernism": "I believe [...] with equally firm faith that the Church [...] was personally instituted by the real and historical Christ when he lived among us, and that the Church was built upon Peter, the prince of the apostolic hierarchy, and his successors for the duration of time" (DS 2145).

9 Translated from the source in Spanish, Catecismo de la Doctrina Cristiana, 57th reprinted edition, Mexico 2001, 39–40.

moved by the Holy Spirit". Those who did not agree with the first statement are not an insignificant number, but almost the other half. This fact is notable. Irrespective from the multiple causes that the respondents could have had to react this way, it is evident that these Catholics (who are neither theologians nor belong to the ecclesial hierarchies) lack a single approach to this matter.

In post-conciliar biblical and theological studies, there is ample consensus that the origin of the church should be understood as a historical/salvific process in which no historical stage or fact, taken separately, gives an account of that origin.[10] Estrada's ecclesiological thinking basically agrees with the consensus mentioned above. In fact, Estrada argues against the approaches that usually interpret the origin of the Church as being the outcome of a particular, historical and quasi-juridical act of the earthly Jesus, losing sight of the Passover experience and the new make-up of the community of followers of Jesus.

In view of that, Estrada's ecclesiology holds a completely opposite approach to locating the origin of the church at a precise point in time. Rather, he remarks on a series of processes and options that under the action of the Spirit led the communities to set up the church and not a sole heterodox intra-Jewish movement.[11] Precisely, an aspect that Estrada likes to underline rather expressly is the active role that the community of disciples had in the emergence of the church as a response to God's initiative as manifested in Jesus under the action of the Spirit:

> *The church has its origin in Jesus, but she is constituted after his death; the church has a Christological dimension, but also a pneumatological and spiritual one; she depends on Jesus' life, but is posterior, apostolic and prophetic; charismatic and institutional as well […].*[12]

In broad terms, Medard Kehl coincides with Estrada: first, Kehl appeals to overcome, as did Vatican II, the reductionist view on the foundation of the church (quite common in post-Tridentine apologetics

10 See the International Theological Comission. [T.N.] The author refers to „La fundación de la iglesia", in: Temas selectos de eclesiología, Madrid 1986, 277–279.

11 See J. A. Estrada, Para comprender cómo surgió la Iglesia, o. c., 63–107.

12 Ibid., 146.

and Neo-Scholasticism) as a juridical-formal act by Christ; likewise, Kehl struggles to get rid of a fundamentalist and ahistorical reading of the Scriptures[13]. Second, Kehl considers the historical theological process of the origin of the church by laying special emphasis on the role played in this process by the Spirit and the community in its variety of self-understandings.[14]

In short, before the Second Vatican Council the opinion held by an immense majority of Catholics, especially by the hierarchy of the church, was that Jesus founded the church in a certain moment during his mortal life. At the beginning of the twenty first century, though, only a 55 % of Catholics in Distrito Federal share this opinion, while almost the other half seems to agree more with the idea that the church has its origin in a decision made by the apostles. Namely, an important part of the population (45 %) seems to coincide with the approach suggested in *Lumen Gentium* and supported by a large number of theologians that the origin of the church has to do with a process. In any case, the difference would be that both the Council and the theologians mentioned do not reduce the origin of the church to a purely sociological process, but it is explained as part of God's salvific plan. In other words, they point out the human and the divine in the origin of the church.

Hence, we are facing a divided idea about the origin of the church. The trouble is not insignificant when we consider that choosing in favour of a certain approach necessarily involves a specific way of understanding the church and consequently the legitimization or delegitimization of certain features, symbols, beliefs and institutional concretions. Certainly, it may be an oversimplification to diminish the many viewpoints about the origin of the Church to only a couple of approaches, particularly having in mind that a more detailed analysis would always manifest several nuances and combinations. Even so, the theoretical and practical verification of at least two approaches tends to reveal one of the causes of the crisis of ecclesial identity nowadays. Two or more different conceptions about the origin involve two or more ecclesial projects or models (which are, to some extent, opposites), which will inevitably stand in tension and rivalry,

13 See M. Kehl, La Iglesia: Eclesiología católica, Salamanca 1996, 70–71.
14 Ibid., 244ff.

especially if one of them becomes hegemonic under the idea of being the only valid one. The above is confirmed by the controversies that arose in this respect within the Church in the post-conciliar period and by the struggle between two ecclesial identities.

* * *

Zusammenfassung zu: José de Jesús Legorreta Zepeda, Die Identität der Kirche

José de Jesús Legorreta Zepeda (México Ciudad | Mexiko) stellt in seinem Beitrag ein Pilotprojekt vor, das den Grad der Übereinstimmung zwischen theologischen Aussagen zur Ekklesiologie und deren Rezeption bei gläubigen Menschen empirisch erheben möchte.

Dieses Projekt geht von der Überlegung aus, dass in sich globalisierenden Gesellschaften homogen-statische Identitäten verschwinden, was auch Auswirkungen auf Institutionen hat. So erweist es sich für religiöse Institutionen als zunehmend schwierig, weiterhin als gesellschaftliche Sinngeber oder als Bewahrerinnen überkommener, starker Identitäten aufzutreten und wirksam zu bleiben. Insbesondere die Katholische Kirche hat von ihren Anfängen bis in die Gegenwart hinein viel Aufwand betrieben, um ihre eigene Identität, sowohl theologisch als auch gesellschaftlich zu stabilisieren und unverändert zu erhalten.

In der Moderne ist Pluralität aber ein unausweichlicher Faktor auch innerhalb der Katholischen Kirche geworden, weswegen das von Legorreta beschriebene Pilotprojekt einen Fokus auf das Kirchenbild von Gläubigen und dessen Übereinstimmung mit dem theologischen Selbstbild von Kirche legt, wobei klar wird, dass bereits bei der Projektkonzeption eine Auswahl aus einer Pluralität von Kirchenbildern getroffen werden muss.

Source/Quelle: José de Jesús Legorreta Zepeda, Identidades eclesiales en disputa: Aproximación "socioteológica" a los católicos de la ciudad de México, Universidad Iberoamericana Ciudad de México – Santa Fé 2006, pp. 51–54 and/und 65–70.]

Thomas Dienberg

Thesenpapier: Orden

„Orden könnten auch heute eine ‚Kirchentherapie' sein. Sie könnten gerade durch ihre prophetische Art, mit den menschlichen Grundsehnsüchten unter den Augen Gottes kulturvoll umgehen, in der Kirche zu einem Wachstum an Mystik, Geschwisterlichkeit und Politik führen.“[1]

Die Ordensgemeinschaften im nord-westeuropäischen Kontext stehen heute vor radikalen Umbrüchen. Die Zahl ihrer Mitglieder nimmt kontinuierlich ab. Klöster werden geschlossen, Provinzen werden fusioniert. Viele Ordensgemeinschaften machen sich von daher auf den Weg der Erneuerung, der Reformierung oder auch des „Refoundings“: Zurück zu den Ursprüngen und dem Charisma der Gründergestalten und der ersten Gemeinschaften. Eine geistliche Erneuerung soll dazu dienen, dass die Orden wieder mehr Strahlkraft haben, wenn sie sich auf ihr Ureigenstes und ihr Charisma rückbesinnen. Für manche Ordensgemeinschaften aber, wie z.B. die Krankenpflegeorden, wird das allerdings schon schwierig. Sie müssen eine ganz neue Mission entwickeln, eine neue Vision erarbeiten und sich damit eine neue Identität geben. Wie aber kann das angesichts der Altersstruktur und der schwindenden Kräfte und Dynamiken überhaupt gelingen? Macht das überhaupt noch Sinn, oder ist es nicht weitaus zukunftsweisender, in Ruhe und Würde als Gemeinschaften zu sterben? Welche Berufung welcher Ordensgemeinschaft heute ist für die Kirche und die Gesellschaft bereichernd und prophetisch?

1 P. M. Zulehner/ J. Haas, Damit die Kirche lebe. Zur Berufung von Ordenschristen in Gottes Kirche heute, Freising 1989, 42.

Ein Teilbereich des Forschungsprojekts zum Thema „Gemeinschaft und Individualismus. Was hält Gesellschaft, Kirche und Orden zusammen?" hat sich ausdrücklich mit der Perspektive der Orden beschäftigt. Der zentrale Punkt der Gemeinschaft in den Orden steht auf dem Prüfstand. Das kann Angst auslösen, denn es impliziert Veränderung und Verwandlung, die man aktiv gestalten sowie passiv erdulden und erleiden muss. Beides ist schwierig. Doch damit sind Ordensgemeinschaften bei weitem nicht allein. Es „zeigt sich bei näherer Betrachtung, dass das Thema Gemeinschaft sowohl im religiös-kirchlichen Kontext wie auch in der sozialpolitischen Diskussion zutiefst ambivalent ist. Die neue Betonung der Gemeinschaft und die Entstehung neuer und intensiver gemeinschaftlicher Lebensformen lösen sowohl Bewunderung und Faszination wie auch Abwehr und Ängste aus."[2]

These 1:

Das Gemeinschaftsleben in Ordensgemeinschaften steht in Frage. Jüngere Mitglieder, so die Ausbildungsverantwortlichen, legen größten Wert auf die Liturgie. Dort erleben sie Gemeinschaft, weniger in der Rekreation und im alltäglichen Miteinander. Das scheint sich mit posttraditionalen Gemeinschaftsformen und Event-Vergemeinschaftungen zu decken. Diese, so Pfadenhauer, geschehen in einer Form sozialer Aggregation, die nicht zweckrational, aber kultisch verortet sind. Der Augenblick und die augenblickliche intensive Hingabe zählen, nicht die solidarisch kontinuierliche Bindung. Interessant ist dabei die Erkenntnis einer Studie, die innerhalb eines Projekts zum Themenkomplex Säkularisierung, Kirche und Orden

2 W. Schaupp, Identitätsfindung in Gemeinschaft, in: K. Schaupp / C. Kunz (Hrsg.), Erneuerung oder Neugründung? Wie Orden und kirchliche Gemeinschaften lebendig bleiben können, Mainz 2002, 41–60, 41f. Vgl. auch den guten Überblick zur Theologie des Ordenslebens von Th. Eggensperger, Anders-Ort Kloster. Perspektiven einer Theologie des Ordenslebens, in: Theologische Revue 112 (2016) 179–190. Eggensperger schließt mit dem Fazit, dass es *ad intra* einer gesunden Spiritualität bedarf, so dass die Klöster anspruchsvolle Anders-Orte sind. *Ad extra* hat das Ordensleben auch einen klaren Verkündigungsauftrag, der für eine Neuorientierung und Rückbesinnung in Theologie und Praxis höchst relevant ist.

in Auftrag gegeben worden ist. Es wird festgestellt, dass die tägliche Eucharistiefeier in Gemeinschaft kein verlässlich konstitutiver Ort mehr zu sein scheint. Hier entsteht ein großes Spannungsfeld innerhalb der Gemeinschaften.[3]

Die Ordensgemeinschaften, so die These, haben ein traditionell festgelegtes weitaus breiteres Verständnis von Gemeinschaft. Wenn sie dieses nicht mehr pflegen, so entsteht aus diesem Glaubensbekenntnis des Individualismus sehr schnell eine Gemeinschaft, die nur noch ‚Momentan-Gemeinschaft' ist, und damit von der Struktur her sehr schnell einer Event-Vergemeinschaftung gleichkommt.

These 2:

Papst Franziskus erwartet von den Ordensleuten im Jahr der Orden:

1. „Wo Ordensleute sind, da ist Freude."
2. Ich erwarte, dass ihr die Welt aufweckt!
3. Ich erwarte daher, dass die Spiritualität der Gemeinschaft … Wirklichkeit wird.
4. Weiter erwarte ich von euch …: aus sich herauszugehen, um zu den existenziellen Peripherien zu gehen.
5. Ich erwarte mir, dass sich jede Form des geweihten Lebens fragt, was Gott und die Menschheit heute verlangen.[4]

Die Gemeinschaft steht in den Aussagen des Papstes zentral, als Gemeinschaft sollen die Ordensleute heute herausgehen und Profil zeigen. Einher gehen diese Aussagen des Papstes mit den Thesen und Aufforderungen, dass die religiösen Gemeinschaften resp. die Ordensgemeinschaften Lebens- und Lernorte von Gemeinschaft werden könnten. Sie können, wenn sie sich erneuern lassen,

3 Vgl., M. N. Ebertz / L. Segler, Orden und Säkularisierung. Ergebnisse aus Befragungen von Mendikanten in Deutschland, Österreich und der Schweiz, Berlin 2015 (Kultur und Religion in Europa Bd. 10), 60.

4 Vgl. Apostolisches Schreiben Seiner Heiligkeit Papst Franziskus zum Jahr des geweihten Lebens, in: http://w2.vatican.va/content/francesco/de/apost_letters/documents/papa-francesco_lettera-ap_20141121_lettera-consacrati.html [Aufruf: 20.07.2016].

Kirchentherapie werden, um es mit den Worten von Zulehner und Haas auszudrücken.[5]

Die These lautet: Ordensleben in Gemeinschaft hat sich auf die ureigenen Werte und Charakteristika zu besinnen und das entsprechend zu leben und mit der Wirklichkeit der Gesellschaft zu konfrontieren. Als Lebensform steht sie in der Spannung von Erneuerung des Charismas und einer zeitgemäßen Interpretation. Nur wer den Mut hat, diese Spannung auszuhalten und auch aktiv anzugehen, wird in der Lage sein, eine Strahlkraft zu besitzen und Menschen heute anzusprechen. Dabei wird es auch wichtig sein, nicht die idealisierte und spiritualisierte Gemeinschaftserfahrung, sondern die realen und begrenzten Gemeinschaftserfahrungen und den Umgang mit diesen Begrenzungen, den Schwachpunkten und dem Sterben in den Blick zu nehmen; entsprechend den Worten des Apostels Paulus: „Wenn ich schwach bin, dann bin ich stark." (2 Kor 2, 10)[6]

These 3:

Es scheint so, als ob die oftmals mittelalterlich geprägten und sich daraufhin entwickelten Gemeinschaftsformen im Orden in der bisher gelebten Form nicht mehr in postmoderner Gesellschaft fortexistieren können. Sterben sie aus? Oder glauben die Ordensgemeinschaften noch immer, dass sie in der Suche nach Gesellschaft und Gemeinschaft heute die Insel der Seligen sind oder sein könnten,

5 Vgl. auch: E. Bianchi, Wir sind nicht besser. Das Ordensleben in der Kirche und inmitten der Menschen, St. Ottilien 2011; M. Gruber / S. Kiechle (Hrsg.), Gottesfreundschaft. Ordensleben heute denken, Würzburg 2007.

6 Ruth Stengel formuliert es wie folgt: „Vor diesem Hintergrund ist zu fragen, wie Ordensleute mit heutigen (Um-)Brucherfahrungen und Enttäuschungen umgehen können. Dabei geht es nicht um die Entwicklung eines spirituellen Expertenprogramms, sondern um ein Tasten im Dickicht der Realität, das die Schwäche und das Brüchige als Ausgangspunkt wählt. (…) Das Unternehmen ist nicht ohne, markiert es doch die aus- und offenzuhaltende Spannung zwischen erlebter und erwünschter Gemeinschaft." R. Stengel, Gemeinschaft als Ideal oder als Realität? Nicht ohne – Überlegungen mit Michel de Certeau SJ, in: Wort und Antwort 56 (2015) 59–64, 62. Die gesamte Ausgabe widmet sich dem Ordensleben mit dem provozierenden Titel: Zeit der Orden? Postmodern reloaded.

wenn sie sich nur auf die Ursprünge und das eigene Charisma besinnen?

Das ‚back to the roots' muss jedoch mit den Zeitströmungen einen konstruktiven Dialog führen, um eine Veränderung um des Lebens und um der Gemeinschaft willen einzuleiten. Das kann zu ganz anderen, neuen, vielleicht auch weniger beständigen Formen von Gemeinschaft führen. Auf einem Workshop mit einigen AusbildungsleiterInnen der Orden wurde folgendes Bild skizziert: Ordensgemeinschaften stellen jeweils Orchester dar, in denen die einzelnen Instrumente und Musiker nicht mehr mit einander harmonieren. Es wird keine gemeinsame Melodie gespielt. Die Individualität und der Individualismus überspielen jeden Versuch einer Re-besinnung auf die gemeinsam vorliegenden Noten.

Charakteristika dafür sind die Parallelwelten und Parallelgemeinschaften im virtuellen Bereich. Die persönliche Begegnung verflacht, die Klagen über Desinteresse am anderen werden immer größer, die ‚rechte Liturgie' steht im Mittelpunk.

Die These lautet: Wenn klösterliche Gemeinschaften sich nicht auf neue und andere Gemeinschaftsformen verständigen, diese einüben und auch von ihren Mitgliedern einfordern, dann wird es sie bald in der west-europäischen Gesellschaft vielleicht nicht mehr geben. Neue und andere Gemeinschaftsformen könnten sein:

- Klösterliches Leben auf Zeit
- Profess auf Zeit
- Anbindung von Menschen ohne Gelübde, die zu bestimmten Zeiten und Phasen im Kloster mitleben
- Gemeinsames Leben von Ordenschristen und Laien, Männern und Frauen, unter einem Dach
- Kommunitäten und kleine Gemeinschaften statt Gemeinschaften in großen Häusern und Konventen, die nur über eine Pforte und ‚jenseits der Mauer' zu erreichen sind (hohe Hemmschwelle)

Ist Mitgliedschaft überhaupt noch ein Modell, das heute trägt? Gemeinschaft heute muss individuell reproduziert werden, jedes Mitglied muss zur Konstitution von Gemeinschaft beitragen. Doch will der Einzelne das heute überhaupt noch? „In dem Maße aber, in dem

Gemeinschaft dergestalt vom Schicksal zur Aufgabe und Zugehörigkeit zu einer Gemeinschaft zu einer Frage der Entscheidung wird, avancieren auch Fragen nach Aufwand und Ertrag zu Kriterien der individuellen Entscheidung für oder gegen die Zugehörigkeit zu einer Gemeinschaft."[7] Was bringt dem Einzelnen ein Eintritt?

These 4:

Ordensgemeinschaften stehen oftmals noch für Werte, die in der Gesellschaft immer mehr ins Hintertreffen geraten. Sie stehen für liebende und solidarische Gemeinschaft – und doch stellt sich die Frage, warum so wenige eine längerfristige Bindung an diese Form von Gemeinschaft suchen. Pfadenhauer stellt fest, dass situative Event-Gemeinschaften eine sehr attraktive Art darstellen, unter spätmodernen Bedingungen Gemeinschaftsgefühle zu erleben. „Die gemeinschaftlichen Erfahrungen von Wärme, Nähe, Direktheit, Unmittelbarkeit und Authentizität, ja von Enthusiasmus und Ekstase scheinen heute – jenseits des Pianissimos einer ‚echten' Liebesbeziehung – fast nur noch auf jene flüchtigen Veranstaltungen beschränkt zu sein, die hier als situative Event-Vergemeinschaftungen bezeichnet werden."[8] Sie stellen Ausnahmesituationen dar, in welchem sich der einzelne, anders als im Einzelkämpferdasein im Alltag, noch als Teil eines Ganzen fühlen darf. „Situative Event-Vergemeinschaftungen lassen sich deshalb als Gemeinschaften ohne Gemeinschaft bezeichnen. (…) Hubert Knoblauch hat vor einigen Jahren klassische posttraditionale Events als strategische Rituale der kollektiven Einsamkeit (…) bezeichnet."[9]

Gemeinsam einsam: Die Stichworte einer illusionären Gemeinschaftsform mit strategischen Ritualen kollektiver Einsamkeit

7 G. Hitzler / A. Honer / M. Pfadenhauer, Zur Einleitung: „Ärgerliche" Gesellungsgebilde?, in: R. Hitzler/ A. Honer / M. Pfadenhauer (Hrsg.), Postraditionale Gemeinschaften. Theoretische und ethnografische Erkundungen, Wiesbaden 2008, 9–34, 11.

8 W. Gebhardt, Gemeinschaften ohne Gemeinschaft, in: R. Hitzler, R. / A. Honer / M. Pfadenhauer (Hrsg.), Postraditionale Gemeinschaften. Theoretische und ethnografische Erkundungen, Wiesbaden 2008, 202–213, 211.

9 Ebd., 212.

können auch für manche Gemeinschaftserfahrungen in den Ordensgemeinschaften stehen. Die Diskrepanz in den Erwartungen an Gemeinschaft zwischen Alt und Jung wird größer. Individualistische Tendenzen erschweren gemeinschaftliche Formen. Tendenzen von außen und von innen führen zu einer ‚gemeinschaftlichen Einsamkeit'. Diese ‚gemeinschaftliche Einsamkeit' zieht kaum Kreise. Wenn das Leben auch im Alltag geteilt wird und Menschen mit in diesen Alltag einbezogen werden, dann hat Gemeinschaftsleben im Orden auf Dauer eine Zukunft und kann auch prophetisch sein. Herzstück sollte dabei die Kontemplation sein, die Einladung suchender Menschen zur Gottesbegegnung in Meditation und Gebet, in der Betrachtung von Welt und Mensch vor Gott.

These 5:

Das ‚Sterben lassen', was sterben will und sterben muss: Ordensleben in Gemeinschaft muss lernen, Abschied zu feiern von Altem und Liebgewordenem, von Traditionen und gemeinschaftlichen Ritualen, die sich sinnentleert haben. Abschied nehmen bedeutet: einen Trauerprozess einzuleiten, etwas begraben, um dann mutig den Weg nach vorne zu gehen und die Zukunft in den Blick zu nehmen.

Es erscheint eine der größten Häresien und Versuchungen in der Kirche wie auch im Ordensleben zu sein, Gott nichts mehr zuzutrauen. Der Gehorsam Gott gegenüber zeigt sich in einem Vertrauen, dass er für den Menschen, für die Kirche und die Ordensgemeinschaft eine Zukunft hat, wenn es auch womöglich eine andere ist, als man sie sich wünscht oder vorstellt. Doch die Wirklichkeit zeigt manchmal anderes: „Bieten wir Christen aber der Welt nicht das peinliche Schauspiel von Menschen, die zwar von Hoffnung reden, aber eigentlich nichts mehr erwarten? (…)"[10]

Zulehner und Haas schrieben bereits im Jahre 1989 folgende heute noch immer geltende Worte: „Als Ordensgemeinschaft Gehorsam lernen, kann auch bedeuten: ‚sterben' lernen. Auch eine Gemeinschaft hat ihre ‚Biographie', ihren Kreislauf von Geburt und

10 J. B. Metz, Zeit der Orden? Zur Mystik und Politik der Nachfolge, Freiburg/Br. 1977, 79.

Tod, von Aufleben und Aussterben, von Blütezeit und Zeit der Erinnerung an sie, von Nachwuchssegen und Nachwuchssorgen. Ständig nach Schuld zu fragen, warum kein Nachwuchs kommt, zermürbt. Fruchtbarer ist es, zur gegebenen Zeit das ‚Nunc dimittis' anzustimmen und zu sehen, dass sterbende Orden Hilfe erhalten, wenn sie ihr Werk aus eigener Kraft nicht mehr schaffen. Solche ‚Sterbehilfe' kann ein Stück Solidarität zwischen Ordensgemeinschaften sein.[11]" J. B. Metz spricht von der charismatischen *ars moriendi* als ein lebendiges Zeichen einer Spiritualität des Loslassens, und er unterscheidet zwischen einer Freiheit und Entscheidung zum Sterben und einem Aussterben.[12] Die Freiheit zum Sterben lassen kann ein prophetisches Zeichen in einer Gesellschaft sein, in welcher nur der Erfolg zählt.

11 P. M. Zulehner / J. Haas, Damit die Kirche lebe. Zur Berufung von Ordenschristen in Gottes Kirche heute, Freising 1989, 44f.

12 J. B. Metz, Zeit der Orden? Zur Mystik und Politik der Nachfolge, Freiburg/Br. 1977, 18ff.

Thomas Dienberg

Research paper: Religious Orders

Even today, religious orders can be therapy for the Church. Under the eyes of God and through their prophetic nature, which consists in addressing the basic human desires and yearnings, they are able to produce growth and maturation in mystic experience, brother- and sisterhood, and politics.[1]

In the context of northwestern Europe, the religious orders are faced with radical change. Their numbers are continuously shrinking. Monasteries and convents are being closed, and territories are fused. Thus, many religious orders have engaged the path of renewal, reform, and "*refounding*": Back to the roots, the charisma of their founders, and the early communities and congregations. A spiritual renewal is expected to renew the radiance of religious orders by re-focusing on their foundation and their original charisma. For some religious congregations however, such as congregations founded for healthcare, this process reveals itself to be not without complications. They have to develop an entirely new mission, a new vision to reinvent themselves. But, given the demographics, how is that even possible because of age, dynamics and dwindling forces? Does it still make sense? Or would it not be more prophetic to slowly die in dignity? What mission of any religious order will reveal itself as enriching and prophetic for the Church?

A part of the research project on "Community and Individualism. What connects Society, Church and Religious Orders?" focused exclusively on the future of the religious orders. The central aspect

1 P. M. Zulehner / J. Haas, Damit die Kirche lebe. Zur Berufung von Ordenschristen in Gottes Kirche heute, Freising 1989, 42.

of community within religious orders is put into question. This can illicit fear and angst since it implies change and reinvention that need to be actively worked for as well as passively suffered through. Both are difficult. But religious orders are not the only ones facing this. "On close examination, the topic community reveals itself as deeply ambiguous – be it in religious-ecclesiastical context or socio-political discourse. The new emphasis of community and the upcoming of new and intense communal life styles evoke admiration and fascination, as well as rejection and fears.[2]

Thesis 1:

The communal life in religious congregations is questioned. According to the educators in charge, younger members have a high appreciation for liturgy. There they experience community much more than in informal gatherings ("Recreation") and in the day to day encounters. This seems in concordance with post-traditional forms of communities and event-specific gatherings. According to Pfadenhauer, they occur in a form of social aggregation not bound to a purpose but have a locus in cult and ritual. What counts is not so much the solidary continuous affiliation, but the moment and the intense commitment at that very moment.[3]

2 W. Schaupp, Identitätsfindung in Gemeinschaft, in: K. Schaupp / C. Kunz (Hrsg.), Erneuerung oder Neugründung? Wie Orden und kirchliche Gemeinschaften lebendig bleiben können, Mainz 2002, 41–60, 41f. Cf. also the excellent summary for the Theology of Religious Life by Th. Eggensperger, Anders-Ort Kloster. Perspektiven einer Theologie des Ordenslebens, in: Theologische Revue 112 (2016) 179–190. Eggensperger draws the conclusion that *ad intra*, a healthy spirituality is required so that monasteries and convents can be appealing Other-Spaces. *Ad extra*, the religious life has a clear mandatory mission that is highly relevant for any attempt for reorientation and reflection on the origins within the theology and practice of the Church.

3 In this context, the conclusion of one study commissioned by the research project for Secularization, Church and Religious orders is very enlightening. It states that the daily Eucharist within the congregation is no longer a reliable locus of constituency. This creates an enormous tension within congregations and religious orders. "This demands an answer as to the necessity of flexibility with regards to the experience of the communal Eucharist as a locus of reliable community facilitating locus within congregations.", in: M. N. Eberts / L. Segler, Orden und Säkularisierung. Ergebnisse aus Befragungen von Mendikanten in

The statement here is: that religious orders and congregations have a broader understanding of community that is traditionally bound. If they don't tend to it, a creed of individualism risks transforming those communities into an "Ad-Hoc-Community" that would not differ at all from any event-congregation.

Thesis 2:

Pope Francis expect from the Religious in the year of the religious orders [2014]:

1) "Where there are religious, there is joy."
2) I am counting on you to wake up the world!
3) I am hoping that the "spirituality of the communion" … will become reality
4) I also expect from you … to come out of yourselves and go forth to the existential peripheries.
5) I expect that each form of consecrated life will question what it is that God and people today are asking of them.[4]

Community is central in the Pope's document. The religious are expected to show themselves as community and establish their profile. The Pope's guidelines are in concordance with theses and requirements for any religious order and/or congregation to become living and learning places and spaces of community. If they are willing to rejuvenate and reinvent themselves, in the language of Zulehner and Haas, they will be able to become therapeutic instrument for the Church.[5]

Deutschland, Österreich und der Schweiz [Religious orders and Secularization. Results and Conclusions from Surveys of Mendicants in Germany, Austria and Switzerland] (Kultur und Religion in Europa Bd. 10), Berlin 2015, 60.

4 Cf. Apostolic letter to all Consecrated People on the occasion of the Year of consecrated life (21. November 2014). http://w2.vatican.va/content/francesco/en/apost_letters/documents/papa-francesco_lettera-ap_20141121_lettera-consacrati.html [Accessed: 07/20/2016].

5 Cf. also E. Bianchi, Wir sind nicht besser. Das Ordensleben in der Kirche und inmitten der Menschen, St. Ottilien 2011; M. Gruber / S. Kiechle (Hrsg.), Gottesfreundschaft. Ordensleben heute denken, Würzburg 2007.

The statement is: Consecrated life in community has to remember and refocus on its very own values and characteristics, to live accordingly, and to confront them with the reality of the society it lives in. As a life style, it finds itself in the tension between renewal of its charisma and its timely interpretation. Only those who have the courage to suffer this kind of tension and deal with it actively in their lives will be able to develop and maintain a radiant force and appeal to the people of today. It will be important not so much to focus on the idealized and spiritualized experience of community but rather the real and limited experiences of community and how to deal with those limits, with weaknesses, and with dying. Guideline might be St. Paul who writes: "For when I am weak, then I am strong!" (2 Cor 12:10, New International Version).[6]

Thesis 3:

Many religious orders have emerged in the middle ages and the forms of community they have developed often seem to adhere to medieval understanding; it seems that they will no longer be able to survive within postmodern society in their traditional form of consecrated communal life. Are they going extinct? Or do religious communities and congregation still believe, that, within the quest for socialization and community today, they can still be the 'Island of the Blessed' if only they focus on their own charisma?

However, any "Back to the Roots" needs to engage in a constructive dialogue with the contemporary currents in order to initiate a change for the sake of life and the community. At a workshop with educators of religious communities, the assessment of the situation

6 Ruth Stengel states: "On this background we must ask how the religious are dealing with today's experience of frictions and fractions and disappointments. This is not about developing a spiritual expertise training but rather to feel one's way in the thicket of reality that starts with the experience of the weak and the fractures. (…) This endeavor is demanding since it delineates the experienced tension between experienced and expected community that needs to be suffered and kept open." R. Stengel, Gemeinschaft als Ideal oder als Realität? Nicht ohne – Überlegungen mit Michel de Certau SJ, in: Wort und Antwort 56 (2015) 59–64, here 62. The entire edition is dedicated to the consecrated life and features the provoking title: Time for the Orders? Postmodern reloaded.

was as such: Congregations of Consecrated Life are like an orchestra in which the instruments and musicians are not in tune. They don't even play the same tune. Individuality and individualism overwrite any attempt at re-orientation to play the sheets music.

Parallel worlds and parallel communities in the virtual realm that often seem more important than the real thing, are characteristics of such a development. Personal encounters become shallow, the complaints of lack of interests in the other come in more frequently, the 'correct liturgy' is in the center instead of sharing the same experiences…

The Thesis is: If religious orders and congregations fail to agree to new and other forms of communities, practice them and hold their members accountable, then there might come a time when they no longer exist in Western European society.

New and other forms of community could be:

- Living in a monastery / congregation for a certain amount time;
- Profession and timely commitment
- Community of People without vows who live in the monastery / congregation for certain times and periods of their lives
- Communal life for religious people and lay people, men and women under one roof
- Communities and small congregations instead of big convents and monasteries that are only accessible by stepping through the big gate to enter the walls (high threshold).

Does membership as a model still work today? Community needs to be recreated on an individual level. Each member needs to contribute to the community. Is that still something that members want to do? "To the degree that community changes from destination for a task and belonging to community to a conscious choice, the notion of effort and return on investment advance to a criterion for the decision of belonging to this community."[7] What does the individual get out of it?

7 R. Hitzler / A. Honer / M. Pfadenhauer, Zur Einleitung: "Ärgerliche" Gesellungsgebilde?, in: R. Hitzler / A. Honer / M. Pfadenhauer (Hrsg.),

Creativity and other forms of belonging might be able to give a boost to the consecrated life and enrich the community. Or has the religious life as it exists today come to its end?

Thesis 4:

Congregations for the consecrated life often still represent values that in society are on the decline. They stand for a loving and solidary community – nevertheless the question is: Why are there so few people who are looking for a long-term commitment to this form of community? Pfadenhauer states that, under postmodern circumstance, ad hoc event communities are very attractive for people who want to experience community. "In these days, the communal experience of warmth, closeness, immediacy, and authenticity, even of enthusiasm and ecstasy seem – beyond the *pianissimo* of a "true" lovers connection – seem to be limited to those fleeting happenings that, here, are referred to as Event-communities [Event-Vergemeinschaftungen]."[8] They constitute exceptions in which the individual, other than the lone survivor in his day-to-day activities, can experience being part of a whole. "Ad hoc Event-Communities can therefore be understood as communities without community. (…) Some years ago, Hubert Knoblauch named classical post-traditional events strategic rituals of collective solitude (…)."[9]

Together lonely: Those notions of an illusionary form of community with strategic rituals of collective solitude could also be used to describe the experience of community in some religious orders and congregations. The discrepancy in their expectations for the community between older and younger members keeps growing. Individualist tendencies make common rituals harder to perform. What remains until the end are the liturgical rituals; not the least reason of which is that fewer members carry the burden of more and more.

Posttraditionale Gemeinschaften. Theoretische und ethnographische Erkundungen, Wiesbaden 2008, 9–34, here: 11.

8 W. Gebhardt, Gemeinschaften ohne Gemeinschaft, in: R. Hitzler / A. Honer / M. Pfadenhauer (Hrsg.), Posttraditionale Gemeinschaften. Theoretische und ethnographische Erkundungen, Wiesbaden 2008, 202–213.

9 Ibid., 212.

There is hardly any time for community left. Influences from the outside as well as from the inside lead to a 'collective solitude'. This 'collective solitude' hardly makes a ripple. Only if life is shared in day-to-day activities and includes people, the community in the religious order will be able to remain prophetic in the future. The core element aught to be contemplation, an invitation to all and any human being on the quest to experience God in meditation and prayer, in contemplation of the world and human beings in the light of God.

Thesis 5:

"Letting die" what wants to die and needs to die: Consecrated life in community needs to learn to say their good-byes to the old and the beloved quaint, to traditions and rituals that have proven to be emptied. Saying good-bye means: to engage in a grieving process, to bury something in order to be able to go boldly ahead and face the future.

It seems to be one of the biggest heresies and temptation within the Church and the religious orders to no longer trust God to do the unexpected. Obedience toward God reveals itself in trusting that God has reserved a future for the Church and consecrated life, even if it is a different one from what people expect of wish for. But reality is different sometimes: "Aren't we Christians presenting to the world the painful drama of people who talk about hope but they don't really expect anything anymore? (...)"[10]

Zulehner and Haas wrote as early as in 1989 the following statement that is still valid: "To learn obedience as a religious order can also mean to learn to die. Even a congregation has its biography, its circle of life in birth and death, in blooming and dying off, in peak and in remembrance thereof, in delighting in newcomers and worries about them. To constantly blame someone or something and ask why there are no new members joining is crushing. It might me more fruitful at a given time to intonate the '*Nunc Dimittis*' and to see that dying orders get help if they are no longer able to fulfill their mission

10 J. B. Metz, Zeit der Orden? Zur Mystik und Politik der Nachfolge, Freiburg/Br. 1977, 79 [engl.: Followers of Christ: The Religious Life and the Church, Mahwah/New Jersey 1978].

on their own. This 'aid in dying' could be an act of solidarity with other congregations."[11] J.B. Metz refers to a charismatic *ars moriendi* as a vital sign of a spirituality of letting go, and he distinguishes between a freedom and a choice to die and a 'dying-off'.[12] The freedom of 'Letting die' could be a prophetic sign in a society where success is the only thing that counts.

11 P. M. Zulehner / J. Haas, Damit die Kirche lebe. Zur Berufung von Ordenschristen in Gottes Kirche heute, Freising 1989, 44f.

12 J. B. Metz, Zeit der Orden? Zur Mystik und Politik der Nachfolge, Freiburg/Br. 1977, 18ff.

Garrett Galvin

Refounding and Reframing Religious Life: Imperatives from the Bible and Early Franciscan Sources

I would like to focus this response on two things: the Incarnation and Individualism. I believe the two things are deeply related and will provide a way forward as we consider this quest for a new "we". Dienberg's paper deeply engages the question of individualism, but I think this question pushes us to a deeper engagement with the idea of Incarnation. The reality of the Incarnation cannot be frozen and each age challenges us to see it in different ways. Just as it was hard for the Pharisees and Sadducees to let go of their ideas of divinity, I think we are a Church struggling to let go of both our Twentieth Century ideas of divinity and religious life.

I was most attracted to the idea of refounding within Dienberg's paper. I would like to approach this idea of refounding by looking at three examples of it in the Bible and then examining one story from the Franciscan tradition that has three iterations. While the Bible cover over a Millennium, these Franciscan stories all come from within a few decades, so it is too much to talk about refounding this early in the Franciscan tradition. In these three iterations, I will try to reveal the necessity of each generation reframing religious life in order to meet the demands of the time in which they are living. Although religious life can become reified into certain habits that have hardened into a distinct and singular form, we actually see a tremendous amount of diversity in our early roots

I would like to look through the lens of the refugee experience in Sacred Scripture in order to understand the quest for a new "we". This is something that Israel has been forced to do repeatedly in its history, and something that we see refugees doing today in many of our own countries. We can think of Abraham as doing this when he left Mesopotamia and came to the Holy Land. We can think of Israel leaving Egypt and refounding itself in the Holy Land with the Torah at its center. Our greatest insight into refugees comes from the treaties that governed relations among the major powers of the ancient Near East. Two classes of refugees emerge from these treaties: political refugees who were nobles and lower-class refugees who were artisans or peasants.[1] If we extrapolate from Hittite treaties,[2] we find that nobles generally could not be extradited, while lower-class refugees like artisans and peasants could.[3] Noble refugees seem to have had great value to foreign kings as possible advisors on their homelands, bargaining chips, or status symbols, but lower-class refugees were often the subject of extradition clauses in these treaties[4] because they had little to offer foreign leaders.[5] The Old Testament witnesses to a new perspective on refugees as the Prophet Jeremiah and ultimately the Prophet Ezekiel challenge the refugees to leave Jerusalem behind and focus on the blessing before them in their new land.

We can think of Israel being brought to Babylon in exile and being urged by the prophet Jeremiah to refound itself there: "Thus says the LORD of hosts, the God of Israel, to all the exiles whom I exiled from Jerusalem to Babylon: Build houses to dwell in; plant gardens, and eat their fruits. Take wives and beget sons and daughters; find wives for your sons and give your daughters husbands, so that they may bear sons and daughters. There you must increase in number, not decrease" (Jer 29:4–6). Two verbs stand out as an essential part of the refounding process: build and plant. As we consider the quest for a new "we", I believe an essential part of that is building and planting.

1 M. Liverani, Runaways and Extradition, in: M. Liverani, International Relations in the Ancient Near East, 1690–1100 Bc (Studies in Diplomacy and International Relations), Basingstone a.o. 2001, 68.
2 R. Westbrook, "International Law in the Amarna Age," in: R. Cohen / R. Westbrook (Eds.), Amarna Diplomacy. The Beginnings of International Relations, Baltimore 2000, 31.
3 G. M. Beckman / H. A. Hoffner, Hittite Diplomatic Texts, (SBL Writings from the Ancient World vol. 7), Atlanta [2nd]1999, 66.
4 D. C. Snell, Flight and Freedom in the Ancient Near East, Leiden a. o. 2001, 87: "International treaties date from the third millennium, and their number grows in the second and first millennia, and a common element is the agreement to return each other's refugees."
5 M. Liverani, Runaways and Extradition, loc. cit. 69.

The key idea here is restoration. Just as Jeremiah encouraged his fellow Israelites to confront the reality of the land in which they were living, I believe his words speak to us today. Religious must build and plant in order to confront the reality of the lands in which they live. Religious life will rise to the challenge of rejuvenation and reinvention in order to become a therapeutic instrument for the Church if it maintains Jeremiah's imperative to build and plant in the times in which it is now living. Rather than doing things as they were done in Jerusalem for Jeremiah's audience or the past for our audience, we must build and plant today.

The final image that I would like to explore from Scripture is the Baby Jesus as a refugee. We discover the Baby Jesus as a refugee in Matthew's Gospel. The Holy Family is a family in flight. Matthew's Gospel describes them as a Judean family who first has to flee to Egypt and ultimately refounds itself as a Galilean family. I include the Holy Family's flight to Egypt as it recalls many of the characteristics of the refugee narratives in the OT that I have just mentioned. We see the importance of the OT, especially for Matthew, for understanding both Jesus and Jesus' world.[6] The connections between Matthew 2:13–15 and the OT have been noted by many scholars: "Just as Israel migrated to Egypt to escape famine, so the Messiah and his family flee to Egypt to escape Herod (2:13–15). Just as God called his son, Israel, out of Egypt, so God calls his son, the Messiah, out of Egypt (2:15)."[7] Just as Moses had to flee Pharaoh, so Jesus had to flee Herod. We discover this refounding process throughout Sacred Scripture.

The refounding of the Holy Family as a Galilean family is an important insight from the recent research on Sacred Scripture. Some argue that the greatest advancement in Christology over the last 25 years is our understanding of Jesus as a Galilean. This is particularly

6 W. D. Davies / D. C. Allison, A Critical and Exegetical Commentary on the Gospel According to Saint Matthew, vol. 3., (International Critical Commentary), Edinburgh 1988, 282: "The importance of the OT for Matthew could hardly be made more evident. One gets the impression that, in his mind, every significant detail of the Messiah's life and ministry could be found – foretold or foreshadowed – in the OT."

7 F. Matera, New Testament Theology: Exploring Diversity and Unity, Louisville 2007, 37.

pertinent to the Gospels of Matthew and Mark. Jesus directs the apostles back to a mountain in Galilee (Mark 14:28; Mt 26:32) in order to meet him after God raises him from the dead. Like being an apocalyptic preacher or being an exorcist, this Galilean prejudice encapsulates another part of Jesus' humanity, which many have tried to downplay or deny in the past. Sacred Scripture forces us to deal with the reality of the incarnation. The Galilean context reinforces Jesus' Jewishness and accentuates Jesus as a special Jew somewhat different from the Jews of Jerusalem. Many who were discontent with the corrupt leadership in Jerusalem had moved to Galilee over the previous century. Some recent scholarship has come to suggest that Galilee could have served as an alternative to Jerusalem for those who believed in the restoration of the patriarchs in the messianic age.[8] Jesus' Jewishness has been attacked on a number of fronts since the Second Century. One of the many problems of the so-called Gnostic Gospels is that along with the humanity of Jesus, his Jewishness disappears.[9] The other extreme, especially in the 19th Century, was to make Jesus Greek. Vestiges of this can be seen in our translation of the New Testament that does not use the Jewish names of the Old Testament: we have Mary instead of Miriam or Jesus instead of Joshua or Matthew instead of Matiyahu. In terms of leadership, this underscores the question of culture once again. This serves as an affirmation of the divine presence not only within humanity, but all cultures of humanity. We live in an age of increasing xenophobia expressed through hatred of immigrants in the United States and much of Western Europe. It should be abundantly clear how counter this is to the Gospels.

We can understand the Holy Family as refounding themselves in Galilee. This was a difficult reality for many Jews as Galilee was generally one of the last places from where a Messiah would be expected to emerge. The Davidic city of Bethlehem is briefly mentioned in the gospels, but not all of them. The reality is that we refer to Jesus as Jesus of Nazareth and not Jesus of Bethlehem. We can see the need

8 S. Freyne, Galilee and Gospel. Collected Essays, Wissenschaftliche Untersuchungen zum Neuen Testament, Tübingen 2000, 256.

9 R. Bauckham, Jesus: A Very Short Introduction (Very Short Introductions), Oxford/New York 2011, 9.

in the Bible to refound and incarnate God's word where it might be most fertile at the time. Jerusalem was controlled by Sadducees, but the Pharisaic movement shared many qualities with Jesus' movement and Galilee may have proved more fertile grounds to start this movement.

After having considered some biblical models, I would like to consider how the Bible is used in the founding and reframing the Franciscan movement. I will consider a story that comes to us from three sources: the Assisi Compilation, 2 Celano, and Bonaventure's *Legenda Maior.* The earliest source seems to be the Assisi Compilation, so we will start there:

> *One time in the very beginning, that is, at the time when blessed Francis began to have brothers, he was staying with them at Rivo Torto. One night, around midnight, when they were all asleep in their beds, one of the brothers cried out, saying: "I'm dying? I'm dying!" Startled and frightened all the brothers woke up.*
> *Getting up, blessed Francis said: "Brothers, get up and light a lamp." After the lamp was lit, blessed Francis said: "Who was it who said, 'I'm dying?'"*
> *"I'm the one," the brother answered.*
> *So that that brother would not be ashamed to eat alone, blessed Francis, a man of great charity and discernment, immediately had the table set and they all ate together with him. This brother, as well as the others, were newly converted to the Lord and afflicted their bodies excessively.*
> *After the meal, blessed Francis said to the other brothers: "My brothers, I say that each of you must consider his own constitution, because, although one of you may be sustained with food less than another, I still do not want one who needs more food to try imitating him in this. Rather, considering his own constitution, he should provide his body with what it needs. Just as we must beware of overindulgence in eating, which harms body and soul, so we must beware of excessive abstinence even more, because the Lord desires mercy and not sacrifice" (Hos 6:6).*

Most critics would agree that the Assisi Compilation is the earliest rendering of this story. It has a number of distinctive elements that ground the story in a different biblical spirituality than the other renderings of this story. Two major elements come out of the story: Francis is recognized as a man of great discernment and the basis of the life is an Old Testament focus on mercy. These only become obvious and noteworthy when we compare them with Celano. When comparing these two texts, Raoul Manselli will argue: "There is, then, a dissimilarity and difference not only in the structure of the discourse, but also in the interpretation of Franciscanism."[10] I will now briefly highlight the dissimilarities and differences.

Second Celano 22:

> *Once they had taken their food in the fear of the Lord, so that nothing would be lacking in this act of charity, the father wove for his sons a long parable about the virtue of discernment. He ordered them to season with salt every sacrifice to God. With concern he reminded them that in offering service to God each one should consider his own strength.*
> *He insisted that it was just as much a sin to deprive the body without discernment of what it really needed as, prompted by gluttony, to offer it too much. And he added: "Dear Brothers, realize that, what I just did by eating was not my own choice, but an exception, demanded by fraternal charity. Let the charity, not the food, be an example for you. For the latter feeds the belly while the former feeds the spirit."*

The first area is the focus on discernment. Francis' gifts of discernment would seem to be much more limited in Celano than the Assisi Compilation. Discernment in Celano would appear to be strictly limited to issues of fasting and gluttony. There is another allusion to discernment when Celano paraphrases John 16:12 where we hear that "each one should consider his own strength." We have a much more robust picture of discernment in the Assisi Compilation. Here Francis is described as "man of great charity and discernment." Many suggest that the earliest writings in the Franciscan Movement begin with a much greater horizon. When comparing the Assisi Compilation to Second Celano, Manselli will point out: "Francis is discerning toward those who went overboard in their asceticism; but he protests those who were disregarding asceticism itself. It is this

10 R. Manselli, "We Who Were With Him: A Contribution to the Franciscan Question," Greyfriars Review 14, St. Bonaventure/New York 2000, 63.

second part that is dropped by Thomas of Celano." As Thomas of Celano is reframing religious life for his different context, he seems to see a need to take some of the edge off of Francis, keep him in line with the religious tradition before him. The radical elements of the Franciscan tradition are picking up steam and some in the movement are starting to see a need to protect the movement from them as they see them as a potentially mortal threat.

The biblical spiritualties embraced by each of these writers tell an important story. I would argue that the Assisi Compilation embraces the most radical spirituality as it paraphrases Hosea 6:6: "the Lord desires mercy and not sacrifice." We can compare this with the scriptural priority of Leviticus and Acts in 2 Celano. The Leviticus paraphrase in 2 Celano may offer a more normative reading and understanding of sacrifice; it states: "season with salt every sacrifice to God." Although this may lighten a sacrifice to a certain extent, it still is using the language of sacrifice. The language of mercy is a major difference to this language.

The concept of mercy is a radical one. We can just look at the most recent Synod in 2015 to see many concerns about mercy as opposed to the consistency of the law. I believe a case may be made for looking upon sacrifices as representing more legal concerns. The Hebrew word behind mercy that we find in Hosea 6:6 is *Hesed.* In his recent book on mercy, Cardinal Kasper describes *Hesed* as such: "*Hesed*, therefore, goes beyond mere emotion and grief at human deprivation; it means God's free and gracious turning toward the human person with care. It concerns a concept of relationship, which characterizes not only a single action, but rather an ongoing attitude and posture."[11] Kasper tell us there are many words for mercy, but "the most important expression for understanding mercy is *Hesed*, which mean unmerited loving kindness, friendliness, favor, and also divine grace and mercy."[12] *Hesed* has an incarnational emphasis that matches many of the early stories of the Franciscans. We can think about Francis' time with the lepers and what a leap of faith that was for him. Michael Blastic tells us: "Francis did mercy with them … he

11 W. Kasper, Mercy: The Essence of the Gospel and the Key to Christian Life, trans. by W. Madges, New York 2014, 43.

12 Ibid.

did not go to the lepers to make himself better, nor did he use them as the object of an ascetical exercise in order to overcome himself (though this is the way his hagiographers will understand Francis' engagement with lepers). Francis is explicit in giving the credit for this experiential truth to God 'The Lord led me among them, and I did mercy with them.'"[13] This has a great sense of *Hesed* within it. Here we see the Incarnation at its strongest.

This emphasis on mercy comes into sharp relief when we compare the biblical references between 2 Celano and Bonaventure. They both seem to move the narrative in more of an ecclesiastical direction. I have already mentioned how Celano uses the language of sacrifice, but he also paraphrases the Acts of the Apostles to offer a setting for this common meal together. Just as the apostles practiced table fellowship in the earliest days of the Church (Acts 2:46), Celano offers the understanding of Francis' outreach to the hungry brother in similar terms. It appears important that Celano offer a biblical defense for the breaking of the fast.

Bonaventure seems to edit this story in a remarkable fashion and moves away from the concerns of the Assisi Compilation. Most would consider this story in the Assisi Compilation and Celano to be a narrative about the "startling austerities of the original Franciscans..."[14] And yet Bonaventure tells this same story in his *Legenda Maior* (5:7), but he changes some significant aspects of it. Bonaventure describes it as an episode of "excessive fasting". Only in Bonaventure's account does just Francis and the hungry brother eat together, we do not find "the rest of the brothers" eating with them as we found in Celano and the Assisi Compilation. We can see both texts doing something vital that we are called to continue doing today: they are both narratives of reframing. Eamon Duffy tells us: "Bonaventure's aim in compiling

13 M. W. Blastic, 'As You Sent Me into the World, So I Sent Them into the World' (Jn 17:18; RnBu XXII:51). Franciscan Evangelical Life and Mission in the Twenty-First Century, in: Th. Dienberg / Th. Eggensperger / U. Engel (Hrsg./ Eds.), Woran glaubt Europa? Zwischen Säkularisierung und Rückkehr des Religiösen / What does Europe believe in? Between secularization and the return of religious life, Münster 2010, 220.

14 E. Duffy, „Finding St. Francis: Early Images, Early Lives", in: P. Biller / A. J. Minnis / E. Duffy (Eds.), Medieval Theology and the Natural Body (York Studies in Medieval Theology), Rochester/New York 1997, 200.

the *Legenda Maior* was to provide an image of the founder which both the advocates of strict observance and their opponents could join in approving, and in this on the whole he succeeded."[15] We see a movement away from the corporate concerns rooted in Celano's allusions to Acts and a shift to another biblical spiritualtiy.

Bonaventure's text in the *Legenda Maior* is more christological. While both texts deal with Sacred Scripture, we see Celano looking at the communitarianism of Acts of the Apostles. Acts 2:46 states: "Every day they devoted themselves to meeting together in the temple area and to breaking bread in their homes. They ate their meals with exultation and sincerity of heart." We see this as a communal act similar to the communal act of Francis and his disciples in Celano's account. Bonaventure explicitly mentions Christ at the end of this story as he connects Francis' actions with Christ's teachings on discernment. "He taught them, moreover, to follow discernment as the charioteer of the virtues, not that which the flesh recommends, but that taught by Christ, whose most sacred live expressed for us the exemplar of perfection."[16] Bonaventure thus returns us to discernment, but this is discernment rooted in following Christ rather than being "a man of great charity and discernment" as in the Assisi Compilation. Bonaventure brings Francis much closer to Christ, an attack on Francis is an attack on Christ. Discernment is vital in the effort to refound religious life. It is something we see being done in these three iterations of the story of the hungry brother, but it is being done by each generation of Franciscans in a slightly different way that is appropriate or seems appropriate to the demands of that age.

Celano focuses on prudence in a manner foreign to Bonaventure's text. We also find a discussion of the Spirit in Celano that is absent in Bonaventure. Celano emphasizes great austerity and focuses on this as an exception. While Bonaventure quotes part of Celano: "Let the charity, not the food, be an example for you," he does not frame this as an exception. According to Eamon Duffy, we can see Celano as offering a subtle warning not to relax the rule.[17] Bonaventure is

15 Ibid.

16 R. J. Armstrong, Francis of Assisi – The Saint (Francis of Assisi: Early Documents vol. 2), New York a. o. 1999, 565.

17 Ibid., 201.

closer to the radical roots of "mercy and not sacrifice" that we find in the Assisi Compilation than to the concerns of trying to fit Franciscan Life into the Church, which were voiced by the Paris Masters to whom Bonaventure may have been responding.

Both Celano and Bonaventure are seeking to reframe religious life. Celano focuses on the communitarianism of Acts and Bonaventure focuses us in a more Christological manner. Both of these are powerful ways to reframe religious life, and they focus on the demands of the incarnation. Something like hunger was a real concern that even Christ faced. We see Christ responding to it at the Feeding of the Four Thousand in Mark and Matthew's Gospel (Mk. 8:1; Mt. 15:32) and the Feeding of the Five Thousand (Mk. 6:30; Lk. 9:11; Mt. 14:12). In many respects Bonaventure can be seen through this Christological lens of concern with hunger over asceticism. We can see this same concern in Marie-Dominique Chenu as he pits the Church's incarnate state against those who would focus "on a one-sided emphasis on individual spirituality and asceticism."[18] Christ recognizes the demands of the incarnation around him. While both the Assisi Compilation and Celano wanted to give room for asceticism, Bonaventure seemed to be concerned with this being used to deny the incarnate. "In Chenu's reading of this history, the inclination long persisted to emphasize the values represented by the eternal, spiritual, the ahistorical, and the abstract, and correspondingly, to neglect the values represented by the temporal, the material, the historical, and the concrete."[19] Chenu returns us to where we started this paper with the concerns of individualism and incarnation.

Individual spirituality and asceticism were in many respects the acceptable elements of religious life in post-Napoleonic Europe. The Franciscan Movement, just like the Jesus Movement, started as a corporate movement with many impacts throughout society. After the secularization and emptying of the convents in the Eighteenth Century, a pious movement seems to have replaced the corporate movement of the original founders and even refounders like St Bernadine

18 C. Potworowski. Contemplation and Incarnation. The Theology of Marie-Dominique Chenu. Mcgill-Queen's Studies in the History of Ideas, Montréal 2001, 159.

19 Ibid., 86.

of Sienna. I think this is the danger of the individualism, upon which Dienberg so correctly concentrates. Chenu focuses us on an incarnation that is both individual and corporate as he warns us about the dangers of a spirituality that drifts off to the ahistorical and abstract. We now live in a Church that shares Chenu's concerns. "The separation of faith and life was in fact the deficit of the incarnation."[20] Concerns about this deficit seem to characterize the papacy of Pope Francis.

Evangelii Gaudium tries to build a bridge between faith and life. As we consider the importance of refounding religious life, *Evangelii Gaudium* reminds us that: "Life grows by being given away, and it weakens in isolation and comfort" (9). The ahistorical and abstract thrive in isolation from the realities of the incarnation, from the realities of every generation trying to re-appropriate the gospel and the values of their religious charism into their own age. *Evangelii Gaudium's* call for the "art of accompaniment" (169) offers a clear answer to the separation of faith and life. This is rooted in mercy, especially that sense of mercy found in *Hesed* that is so important at the beginning of the Franciscan Movement in Hosea 6:6. The deficit of incarnation is truly a deficit of mercy. As we try to refound religious life and face the challenges of a new generation and new technology, let us remember the words at the closing of *Evangelii Gaudium:* "Let us not say, then, that things are harder today; they are simply different. But let us learn also from the saints who have gone before us, who confronted the difficulties of their own day. So I propose that we pause to rediscover some of the reasons which can help us to imitate them today" (196).

***

20 Ibid., 126.

Zusammenfassung zu: Garrett Galvin, Neubegründung und Neuausrichtung des religiösen Lebens. Imperative aus der Bibel und aus frühen franziskanischen Quellen

Garret Galvin (Oceanside, CA | USA) sieht in einer erneuerten Verbindung von Individualismus und inkarnatorischem Denken einen Weg in Richtung eines neuen Wir. Um diese Verbindung heute begründen und neu ausrichten zu können führt er eine Relecture von drei biblischen Texten und drei auf diesen aufbauenden Quellen des frühen Franziskanerordens durch, anhand derer er aufzeigt, wie jede Generation religiöses Leben kontextualisieren muss, um den Anforderungen ihrer Zeit gerecht zu werden.

Aus dieser Verbindung und insbesondere aus einem inkarnatorischen Denken geht für Galvin auch eine Warnung vor den Gefahren einer ahistorischen und abstrakten Spiritualität hervor, da inkarnatorisches Denken und Glauben, mit Marie-Dominique Chenu gesprochen, immer einen individuellen und gemeinschaftlichen Aspekt aufweist. Deswegen kann inkarnatorisches Denken auch einem Dualismus von Glaube und Leben vorbeugen.

Hierin sieht Galvin ein besonderes Anliegen von Papst Franziskus, der die individuelle und gemeinschaftliche Doppelstruktur des Glaubens im Terminus der Barmherzigkeit ins Zentrum rückt – ein Anliegen, das auch am Anfang des Franziskanerordens stand.

Franziska Madl

Das Anziehende ist immer das Lebendige

Bei den folgenden Anfragen an das Thesenpapier von Thomas Dienberg handelt es sich um echte kritische und weiterführende Fragen, die ich mir selbst immer wieder stelle – und die ich mir auch gemeinsam mit unserer Formationsgemeinschaft gestellt habe.

1. Was meint „Rückbesinnung auf das eigene Charisma"?

Nicht erst seit dem Zweiten Vatikanischen Konzil wird immer wieder eine Rückbesinnung auf die ureigenen Werte und Charakteristika der Orden eingefordert. Den Konzilsvätern ging es um eine Erneuerung des Charismas und eine zeitgemäße Interpretation desselben: „Zeitgemäße Erneuerung des Ordenslebens heißt: ständige Rückkehr zu den Quellen jedes christlichen Lebens und zum Geist des Ursprungs der einzelnen Institute, zugleich aber deren Anpassung an die veränderten Zeitverhältnisse." (Perfectae caritatis, Nr. 2)

Die Rückkehr zu den Quellen könne und werde den Orden wieder Strahlkraft geben. Aber reicht diese viel beschworene Forderung allein aus, ohne weiter zu fragen: Was gehört denn *konkret* zu diesen ureigenen Werten, zu diesem ureigenen Charisma? Wo sind die Quellen, zu denen wir zurückkehren sollen – und wie sehen sie aus?! (Da gehen die Vorstellungen und Erwartungen in unseren Gemeinschaften extrem weit auseinander. Und oft stellt sich die Frage auch sehr reduziert: Habit – Nachwuchs?)

Im Thesenpapier von Thomas Dienberg wird das Beispiel der Krankenpflegeorden genannt, die sich heute eine neue Identität geben müssten. Aufgrund der Altersstruktur und der schwindenden Kräfte der Gemeinschaften scheint sei dies jedoch sehr schwer oder kaum möglich. Die alten (bzw. älteren) Orden, die keinen so eng gefassten und konkret formulierten Auftrag haben, scheinen es im Vergleich dazu *leichter* zu haben. (Vgl. die Aufstellungsübung im Lehrgang „Verantwortung in religiösen Gemeinschaften"[1]: Was haben die alten Orden den jüngeren Gemeinschaften zu sagen und umgekehrt? Was ist das Geheimnis des Altwerdens? Ein möglichst offener und breiter Gründungsauftrag.) So kann man etwa in unserem Orden immer wieder hören, der Predigerorden sei allein schon deshalb „immer aktuell" und „immer lebendig", weil es der Glaubensverkündigung einfach immer und überall bedarf (heute vielleicht sogar mehr denn je). Dominikanerinnen und Dominikaner seien deshalb so vital, weil unser Ordensauftrag so weit abgesteckt ist, dass fast alles reinzupassen scheint. Das ist nicht falsch. Aber ist das wirklich so einfach? Kann eine solche These manchmal nicht auch bloß eine bequeme Entschuldigung oder Ausrede darstellen, die hilft weiteren Fragen aus dem Weg zu gehen? Vor allem der Frage, was das ganz konkret für uns hier und heute bedeutet?

Beim Workshop der Ausbilderinnen und Ausbilder in den Mendikantenorden, der im Rahmen des Forschungsprojekts „Gemeinschaft und Individualisierung. Was hält Gesellschaft und Kirche zusammen?" im Herbst 2015 in Köln stattfand, ist in der Diskussion der schöne Satz gefallen: „Man kann sich auch ganz gut hinter der eigenen Ordenstradition verstecken." Gemeint war das als kritische Rückfrage an Öffentlichkeitsarbeit und Berufungspastoral; diskutiert wurde das Image, das Bild der Gemeinschaft, welches wir im Rahmen von Öffentlichkeitsarbeit und Berufungspastoral „verkaufen". Wie sehr wird in entsprechenden Webauftritten und Broschüren die Ordens-„Idee" überhöht und damit losgelöst von der konkreten Gemeinschaft vor Ort? Die meisten jungen Menschen, die heute zu uns kommen und eintreten möchten (eigentlich alle), haben sich vorher durch Literatur und über das Internet informiert. Bei ihrem Besuch im Kloster werden sie dann mit der konkreten Ordensrealität konfrontiert. Wenn dann Ideal und Realität zu weit auseinander klaffen, wird es schwierig …

Für uns Dominikanerinnen kommt noch verschärfend die Frage hinzu: Was bedeutet es heute, *Frau zu sein* im (Prediger-)Orden? Da liegt richtig viel Arbeit vor uns, denn die alten Plausibilitäten

1 Vgl. http://www.kardinal-koenig-haus.at [Aufruf: 14.01.2017].

funktionieren nicht mehr; vor allem Rollenbilder und Erwartungen haben sich stark verändert. Schwestern sind nicht einfach die „weibliche Version" der Brüder!

2. Tradition und/oder Traditionen (Marie-Dominique Chenu OP)

Es ist richtig, dass Ordensgemeinschaften lernen müssen, „Abschied zu feiern von Altem und Liebgewordenem, von Traditionen und gemeinschaftlichen Ritualen, die sich sinnentleert haben" (These 5: „Sterben lassen"). Aber das ist genau der Punkt, an dem wir extrem vorsichtig sein und gut zu unterscheiden lernen müssen, um nicht das Kind mit dem Bade auszuschütten. Wir müssen uns immer wieder selbstkritisch die Frage stellen: Was hat sich *wirklich* sinnentleert? Was war denn der ursprüngliche Sinn dieser Regel und jener Vorschrift? Können wir statt dessen eine neue, angemessenere Form finden, oder werfen wir einen alten Usus (un-)gerechtfertigterweise über Bord? Warum tauchen in Gemeinschaften mit jungen Brüdern und Schwestern immer wieder Dinge oder Verhaltensweisen auf, die die älteren und alten Schwestern oder Brüder seit Jahrzehnten für definitiv abgehakt gehalten haben? Und welche Bedeutung haben diese Wiederentdeckungen – gerade dort, wo es sich nicht bloß – was auch vorkommt – um naiv-ästhetizistische Traditionsverliebtheiten handelt, sondern es um ein echtes Ringen um die Tradition geht?

Mein persönliches Lieblingsbeispiel hier ist das Schuldkapitel. Ein gemeinschaftliches Ritual, das man – weil es als sinnentleert erfahren wurde – ersatzlos gestrichen hat. Aufgrund der eigenen schlechten Erfahrungen war man nicht willens oder in der Lage, neue Formen der *Versöhnung in Gemeinschaft* zu finden. Nun aber stellt sich die Frage: Wie gehen wir heute mit Schuld und Verletzungen in Gemeinschaft um, wie kommt man zu Versöhnung auf gemeinschaftlicher Ebene? Gibt es neue Formen dafür – und kann man aus der *ursprünglichen* Intention und Form des Schuldkapitels etwas für heutiges kommunitäres Leben *wieder*gewinnen? Mit diesen Fragen hat sich beispielsweise das jährliche Treffen junger Dominikanerinnen in Europa im Januar 2015 drei ganze Tage lang beschäftigt – sehr zum Entsetzen vieler älterer Mitschwestern in unseren Gemeinschaften.

Wir verwechseln wahrscheinlich oft unsere Tradition mit unseren Traditionen. „Die Tradition ist keine Ansammlung von einzelnen Traditionen, sondern ein Prinzip von organischer (…) Kontinuität…“[2]. Wir täten gut daran, hier besser und sauberer zu unterscheiden. Was kann weg – aber was muss bleiben? Ein Orden muss „Kontakt halten mit seinen Ursprüngen“ und „Anschlussfähigkeit von gestern nach morgen herstellen“. Michael Hochschild nennt das „elastische Tradition“. Für Orden, denen das nicht gelingt, verwendet er ein recht abschreckendes Bild: „Man könnte den Orden von heute dann […] mit einem aufgeschreckten Huhn vergleichen, dem man (mit seiner Tradition) den Kopf abgeschlagen hat, das aber noch eine Weile herumrennt, um dann tot umzufallen.“[3]

3. Keine Bindung auf Dauer mehr? Oder: Die „Magie der Zahl“

Eine Bindung auf Dauer gehört auch für jüngere Ordensleute ganz wesentlich zur *vita consecrata* dazu, eben weil es sich um eine *Lebensform* handelt, nicht um ein „Praktikum“, einen „Job“ oder eine „Auszeit zur Selbsterfahrung“. Es geht ihnen tatsächlich um „Berufung“ und „geweihtes Leben“. Sie sehen die Profess durchaus als ein „Wagnis“ an, die Notwendigkeit der Bindung als eine „Hürde“ im positiven Sinn (die außerdem jene fernhält, die eigentlich etwas anderes suchen). Die Strahlkraft des Ordenslebens sehen sie oft gerade in dieser Notwendigkeit einer Bindung auf Dauer. Zur Gemeinschaftserfahrung gehören für sie deshalb auch Haltungen und Überzeugungen wie z. B.: „zum eigenen Wort stehen“; „das Versprechen als Zeugnis“; „gemeinsam etwas durchstehen, ohne gleich davonzulaufen“, etc.

2 M.-Dominique Chenu, Le Saulchoir. Eine Schule der Theologie. Aus dem Französischen von M. Lauble, von Institut M.-Dominique Chenu – Espaces Berlin durch C. Bauer / Th. Eggensperger / U. Engel (Hrsg,) (Collection Chenu Bd. 2), Berlin 2003, 133.

3 M. Hochschild, Elastische Tradition. Biometrie des Klosters von heute (Studien zur monastischen Kultur), St. Ottilien 2013, 104.

Gehören Werte wie Beständigkeit und Treue nicht ganz *zentral* zum Charisma des Ordenslebens? Gäbe man mit ihnen nicht etwas Konstitutives auf? Wofür? Beim Vorschlag neuer Gemeinschaftsformen muss man die kritische Rückfrage stellen dürfen, welches Ziel damit tatsächlich verfolgt wird. Wenn es sich um pastorale Ziele in Ausübung des Ordensauftrages handelt, ist eine große Bandbreite an Möglichkeiten denkbar. Wenn es aber eigentlich (nur) um das Generieren von Nachwuchs geht (nach dem Motto, es würden wieder mehr eintreten, wenn sie sich nicht auf Dauer binden müssten), tun sich neue Problemfelder auf. Man wird sich dann fragen müssen: „Welche Leute ziehen wir damit an?“ Und: Führte eine solche Strategie letztlich nicht dazu, „unsere Form unseres Ordenslebens“ aufzulösen?

Ich persönlich hege den Verdacht, dass das Problem eigentlich anderswo liegt, nämlich bei der Verwechslung von Qualität und Quantität und damit in der Frage nach neuen Gemeinschaftsgrößen und -strukturen. Dahinter steckt die oft lähmende „Magie der Zahl“. Diese Magie lässt uns auf Statistiken und Zahlen starren, die uns jährlich präsentiert werden und den Niedergang der Orden auch graphisch darstellen. Letztlich paralysiert uns diese Zahlenmagie! Sehr verräterisch ist in diesem Zusammenhang das Wörtchen *„noch“*: „Wir sind *noch* 21 Schwestern.“, „Wie viele Mönche leben *noch* in diesem Stift?“, „Wie viele Schwestern seid ihr *noch* in der Schule?“, „Habt ihr *noch* Nachwuchs?“, usw. Der Blick allein auf sinkende Zahlen und schwindende Bastionen ist nicht wirklich zielführend. Das ist das Bild, das wir von uns selbst haben und auch nach außen transportieren (etwa auch bei Pressekonferenzen).

Michael Hochschild stellt (mit Blick auf jene Benediktinerklöster, die er für seine Studie soziologisch untersucht hat) fest: „Ob der Abt nun viele oder wenige Mönche hat, ist für die Lebensqualität des Klosters heute anscheinend eine vordringliche Frage. Aber die entscheidende Frage ist eine andere: *ob und wie es mit vielen oder auch mit wenigen Mönchen gelingt, diese Qualität (vor) zu leben beziehungsweise zu gestalten*. Wer in einer kleinen Gemeinschaft lebt und arbeitet, kann sich ein anonymes Leben wie in einer großen Gemeinschaft nicht erlauben, ohne dass die Gemeinschaft, ihr Sinn und Zusammenhalt darunter leiden. Es wäre ein Irrtum zu glauben, ein für eine große Mönchsgesellschaft angelegtes Kloster könnte nicht auch von einer kleinen Gemeinschaft genutzt werden, und das Kloster bräche zusammen, weil es an purer Masse fehlte. (Mit dem statistischen Rückgang in den Klöstern geraten die zunehmend vor die Frage, wie sie aus der *massebedingten Gesellschaftsform ihrer Geschichte wieder in Vergemeinschaftungsstile* zurückfinden.) [...] Die Kirche im Allgemeinen wie die Orden im Besonderen müssen im 21. Jahrhundert daraus eine Selbsterkenntnis machen und *veränderten Gruppengrößen* in ihrem eigenen Lebensraum Rechnung tragen. In der aktuellen Umbruchsituation der Klöster fehlt es am Verständnis dafür, dass man als kleine Gemeinschaft nicht wie eine große Gesellschaft zusammenleben kann, dass die *Verbindlichkeiten* zunehmen und die *Rollen(-probleme)* bedeutsamer, weil sichtbarer werden. Kurzum: dass es mit den verkleinerten *Gemeinschaften ein neues Maß der Dinge* gibt – nur welches?"[4]

Diese Entwicklung muss Auswirkungen haben auf Berufungspastoral und Formation: In kleineren Gemeinschaften „treten die Stärken und Schwächen der Einzelnen stärker hervor"[5], d.h. man muss mehr Vorsicht bei Auswahl und Zulassung walten lassen als früher. Zugleich schaukeln sich die gegenseitigen Erwartungen hoch.

4. Die veränderte Rolle der Arbeit und ihre Auswirkungen auf Gebet und Gemeinschaft

Beim Ausbildungsleiterworkshop im letzten Herbst haben wir uns auch kurz die Frage nach dem Verhältnis von Gemeinschaft und Arbeit gestellt: Wo liegt der Schwerpunkt? Eine der Wortmeldungen, die ich mir damals notiert habe, lautete: „Mich in der Arbeit verwirklichen kann ich überall, deshalb suche ich mir keine Gemeinschaft, sondern ich tue das, weil ich ein bestimmtes gemeinschaftliches Leben vorfinden will [...] und dann kommen all diese Fragen nach den konkreten Bedingungen des Alltags. Für Schwesternkongregationen kommt oft noch die Frage nach den Werken hinzu, in denen die Schwestern seit Generationen traditionell tätig

4 Ebd., 108f.
5 Ebd., 106.

waren – v. a. wenn die Jungen gar kein Interesse an diesen Werken haben."

Michael Hochschild nennt das, was derzeit in vielen Klöstern passiert, sehr treffend die „monastische Kunst, sich zu Tode zu leben": „Normalerweise reagieren die Klöster auf ihre heutige Umbruchsituation mit einer ‚Kunst, sich zu Tode zu leben': Sie verteilen die Arbeitslast auf immer weniger Schultern und gefährden schon dadurch die seelische Hygiene ihrer Mönche wie des Klosters. Die Betriebsamkeit nimmt unaufhörlich zu […]. Selbst kontemplative Klöster geraten in Bewegung, ja unter Druck."[6] Hochschild warnt vor der realen Gefahr, von außen gar nicht mehr als Kloster wahrgenommen zu werden, sondern eher als „pseudoreligiöser Hochleistungsbetrieb"[7]. Die Rolle der Arbeit und das Arbeitsklima haben sich auch in den Ordensgemeinschaften durch die digitale Revolution sehr verändert – hier unterscheiden wir uns nicht von unseren Mitmenschen „da draußen". Es gibt keinen klaren Anfang und kein klares Ende der Arbeit, sondern wir sind eigentlich rund um die Uhr beschäftigt, nicht zuletzt auch weil die Umwelt uns ständig anfragen kann (per Handy, Mail,…) – auf Kosten des Schlafes und auf Kosten des Gebetes. (Gleichzeitig verkaufen sich die Klöster nach außen aber oft als Oasen der Stille.) Hochschild rät den Orden daher dazu, eine „neue Haltung der spirituellen Souveränität"[8] aufzubauen und gerade im Kloster die meist offene Frage (neu) zu klären, wann die Arbeit denn eigentlich erfolgreich war und wann sie als beendet gilt – gerade auch wegen ihrer Auswirkungen auf den Einzelnen und die Gemeinschaft. In vielen Klöstern scheint die Gefahr zu bestehen, nur noch über die Arbeit Gemeinschaftserfahrung herstellen zu können. Die Frage ist dann auch, wie es gelingen kann, innerhalb der Gemeinschaft das Arbeitsethos der Älteren mit dem Wunsch nach Work-Life-Balance der Jüngeren zusammenzubringen, ohne dass man sich ständig gegenseitig Vorwürfe macht.

6 Ebd.
7 Ebd., 167
8 Ebd., 45

5. Freiheit zum Sterben und/oder doch Freiheit zum Leben?

Kann es sein, dass die Orden (wie die Kirche) sich die Krise und das Sterben auch ständig selbst einreden und herbeireden? Da gibt es ganz viel Trauer und Schmerz darüber, dass es nicht mehr ist, wie es früher einmal war. Selbst wenn man das durchschnittliche Maß an Vergangenheitsverklärung abzieht, bleibt immer noch dieser paralysierte Blick auf Zahlen und Statistiken. Das Dauergerede von der Krise lähmt uns einzeln und als Gemeinschaften. Sind Klöster wirklich nicht mehr als ein Auslaufmodell aus längst vergangener Zeit und daher alle zum Sterben verurteilt? Was ist mit jenen Gemeinschaft, die noch leben können und wollen? (vgl. das recht einseitige Fortbildungsangebot für Ordensleute in Österreich und Deutschland: Da gibt es viele Seminare und Kurse über das Altwerden, das Schließen von Werken und Klöstern, das Hereinnehmen von Laien in die Verantwortung,… aber im Verhältnis dazu sehr wenig über Berufungspastoral, Formation und sinnvolle, altersgemäße Lebensgestaltung für jüngere Ordensleute.)

Was macht es mit jungen Ordensleuten, wenn sie von Anfang an ständig nur hören, dass sie zu einer aussterbenden Spezies gehören, dass „eh alles den Bach runter geht", dass wir nur noch gemeinsam unseren würdevollen Abgang vorbereiten können.

Ja, es braucht die Freiheit zum Sterben – wir müssen Tradition*en* sterben lassen (mit der gebotenen Vorsicht, damit nicht unsere Tradition mitstirbt); und es werden auch Gemeinschaften sterben müssen und dürfen (mit der nötigen Ruhe und Würde). Wir haben aber als Ordensgemeinschaften aus unserem „Gottesoptimismus" heraus auch eine große Widerstandsfähigkeit. Wo bleibt unser Lebenswille? Für mich selbst, für meine eigene Gemeinschaft – und für alle jungen Ordensleute, egal wo und wie sie sich auf dieses Abenteuer einlassen wollen – wünsche ich mir aber die Freiheit zum Leben! Denn, wie Erich Fromm es so schön formuliert hat: „Das Anziehende ist immer das Lebendige." Oder ganz biblisch aus dem Buch der Weisheit: „Gott hat den Tod nicht gemacht und hat keine Freude am Untergang der Lebenden" (Weish 1,13).

* * *

Summary: Franziska Madl, It is the vibrant that appeals.

Franziska Madl (Vienna | Austria) considers the necessary conditions for the successful modernisation of life in religious orders. She focuses on the one hand on what form a vitalising return to the origins of an order might take, and on the other on how community life can be shaped for the future without a community hiding behind its own tradition. Madl stresses that although it is important to let go of empty rituals and traditions, there is as yet no consensus on just which rituals and traditions this involves.

This question of letting go also has practical implications for life together within ever smaller communities, as that change in size changes the dynamics: the strengths and weaknesses of the individuals emerge more clearly, and at the same time, community members' mutual obligations and expectations of each other grow and role problems can occur. The result is new demands in terms of vocational pastoral care, life-sharing between different generations and the areas in which religious orders work.

Madl concludes by advocating an optimism in God which can, even in difficult circumstances, produce a resilience and an appealing freedom to live within religious orders.

Joseph P. Chinnici

On a Quest for a new 'We': A Gospel Response

I am very pleased to be able to write a response to this stimulating reflection by Thomas Dienberg, a brother and colleague in the Franciscan family. The major theme of the project is "Community and Individualism. What connects Society, Church and Religious Orders." Five theses are presented for consideration, reflective of the religious life in northwestern Europe. I would like to begin by summarizing these in my own words. The summary is, at the same time, an interpretation:

1. The understanding of community within religious orders is much broader than the current modern and post-modern attempt to from "ad-hoc event communities" around ritual and cultic experiences that are intense, immediate, and transitory.
2. The ecclesial expectations for religious place them in a tensive situation which demands that they not retreat into a "cloistered" utopianism but engage the present situation in all of its limitations and challenges.
3. New forms of community that break from traditional patterns are needed to engage the world on its present terms. Key to these forms will be a sense of communal belonging engendered by conscious choices by individual persons.
4. A "collective solitude" is one hallmark of these "ad-hoc event communities". If traditional forms are to survive at all, what is needed is to break from this emergent experience and to engage others in a daily routine of interaction in work, play, projects, and above all prayer if traditional forms are to survive.

5. God's future for religious life requires trust that new forms will develop under God's guidance, and in this light, inherited forms of life and the people who embody them must cease worrying about membership and embrace the transitoriness of their practice and understanding. They need at times to engage in a collective *ars moriendi* that in itself sets a foundation for thc futurc.

Professor Dienberg's reflections are extremely valuable for placing the trends within religious life in a larger social and intellectual context, that of modernity and post-modernity. The challenges come from the interchange between the *without* in society and the *within* in religious life. They emerge from the context of an inculturated life-experience marked by individualism, immediacy, transitory forms of consumption, and the disappearance of collective forms of solidarity: memory, inheritance, socially embodied traditions in formation and education, collective works. At the same time they clearly reflect a search for community and the development of new "therapies of the soul". These trends are particularly representative of the developed world. For religious life to develop, the challenges must be faced, the good sorted from the not-so-good, and a new, visible, and enacted public performance developed. The methodology of the paper takes culture seriously and follows the relationship between the Church and the world outlined in *Gaudium et Spes* 40–44. Religious life, inheriting a model separating itself from the world, is not immune to this new model of inter-penetration between religion and society. It is to Dr. Dienberg's great credit that he analyzes the current situation from this perspective. Only if we place the *within* and the *without* in the same interactive field, their mutual interpenetration, can we even begin to identify the key elements of new forms.

The situation in the United States is somewhat similar to that described for Europe.[1] Robert Wuthnow, one of the premier sociol-

1 Cf. for example the analysis of the situation in Germany, Switzerland, and Holland in terms of the collapse of the "Catholic milieu", a situation very similar to the fashioning in the United States of Cold War Catholicism and its subsequent collapse: M. E. Ruff, The Wayward Flock: Catholic Youth in Postwar West Germany, 1945–1965, Chapel Hill/North Carolina 2005. On the European experience see: J.-L. Ormières, L'Europe désenchantée, La fin de l'Europe chéetienne?

ogists of religion in the United States, has described the movement since the 1950s as one from "a spirituality of dwelling" (marked by sacred place, security, status, roles, hierarchies) to "a spirituality of seeking" (marked by sacred moments, pilgrimage, journey, loneliness). His call is for a return to religious practices embedded in social institutions.[2] The erosion of the traditional approach is due in large measure to the dominant consumer, market, and entitlement society developed in the United States, now aided by the technological revolution. A study of young adult Catholics born between 1960–1980 indicates a strong attention to spirituality, a thirst for real presence, and a commitment to peace and global dimensions of Catholicism. All of these elements are mixed with *anomie* with respect to ecclesial belonging. There is declining institutional affiliation and a corresponding commodification of religious experience.[3] The impact of these trends on religious vocations, although there is no completely uniform picture of decline, can be easily seen in a succession of statistical reports from the Center for Applicate Research in the Apostolate (CARA, Georgetown University).[4] The United States remains a religiously diverse country and is marked by a certain spiritual vitality, differentiating it from its European counterparts. Nevertheless, many similar elements join the two experiences, and from this point of view Dienberg's theses with respect to Europe seem to this author to correspond in some measure to what is happening in religious life in the United States.

France, Belgique, Espagne, Italie, Portugal, Fayard 2005. For comparative studies using different terms to describe the changes in the relationship between Christianity and society, see N. Christie / M. Gauvreau (Eds.), The Sixties and Beyond, Dechristianization in North America and Western Europe, 1945–2000, Toronto 2013.

2 R. Wuthnow, After Heaven. Spirituality in America Since the 1950s, Berkeley 1998.

3 D. R. Hoge / W. D. Dinges / M. Johnson/ J. L. Gonzales, Young Adult Catholics: Religion in the Culture of Choice, Notre Dame 2001.

4 CARA special reports include: Population Trends Among Religious Institutes of Women I, Fall 2014, http://cara.georgetown.edu/WomenReligious.pdf [Accessed: 04/21/2017], Religious Institutes of Men Trends Special Report Fall 2015, http://cara.georgetown.edu/ReligiousMenSpecialReport.pdf [Accessed: 21.04.2017]; Nurturing Vocations to Religious Life and Priesthood, Spring 2014, http://cara.georgetown.edu/publications/NurturingVocations.pdf [Accessed: 04/21/2017].

It is at this point that I would like to change the methodological starting point for envisioning the future and seeing how society, Church, and religious orders might intersect. The patterns indicated from the sociological point of view are evident and identifiable; but after the social analysis, what next? It may very well be true that the social analysis approach, as strong and valuable as it is, will not clarify the situation as to the future emergence of a viable religious life. The forces of modernity and post-modernity, including globalization and technology, are simply too dissolving of traditional life-forms, constraints, and absolutes, particularly in the European-American axis, to allow inherited concepts of religious life to thrive.[5] Here I want to elaborate on Dr. Dienberg's reference to Pope Francis (thesis 2) and to the necessity of contemplation (thesis 4). Perhaps we need to approach the issue of the future of the relationship between the Church, society, and religious life from the viewpoint of these more charismatic and evangelical elements. Perhaps in trying to divine the future, we need self-consciously to prepare for a deeper reliance on those most elusive of sociological phenomena, grace, faith, and conversion. The difficulties of today are the breeding ground for the faith of tomorrow.

When drafting the Aparecida document for the Latin American Episcopal Conference, Cardinal Bergoglio made a significant anthropological shift. As narrated by his biographer, Bergoglio insisted that the document not begin with social analysis, as had been the typical approach of the "see, judge, act" method of inquiry.[6] Rather, he wished to define how the world is seen from the evangelical experience of God's love. The final document makes a subtle but significant change from the traditional interpretation: "In continuity with the previous general conferences of Latin American Bishops, this document utilizes the see-judge-act method. *This method entails*

5 See in this context the descriptions comparing trends in the northern and southern hemispheres offered in J. Allen, The Future Church. How Ten Trends are Revolutionizing the Catholic Church, New York 2009. For globalization see also T. Howland Sanks, "Globalization and the Church's Social Mission", Theological Studies 60 (1999), 625–651; R. J. Schreiter, The New Catholicity: Theology between the Global and the Local, Maryknoll/New York 1997).

6 For background see A. Ivereigh, The Great Reformer: Francis and the Making of a Radical Pope, New York 2014, 294–301.

viewing God with the eyes of faith through his revealed word and life-giving contact with the sacraments, so that in everyday life we may see the reality around us in the light of his providence, judge it according to Jesus Christ, Way, Truth, and Life, and act from the Church, the Mystical Body of Christ and the universal Sacrament of salvation, in spreading the kingdom of God which is sown on this earth and fully bears fruit in Heaven." (n. 19) This same starting point for contemporary analysis is consistently present in the *Exhortation* following the Synod on the New Evangelization, the Encyclical letter on environmental concerns, and the exhortation *Amoris Laetitia*.[7] For Pope Francis it may be traced to the starting point elucidated most formally in the *Exercises* of Ignatius Loyola. But this transcendental foundational experience was also the analogous starting point for the response of the great fashioners of a cohesive religious response to the equally confusing experiences of their times: Augustine to the experience of social and cosmic disorder; Benedict to the problems of class division; Francis to the challenge of the commercial society and the opacity of the Church; Francois de Sales and Jeanne de Chantal to the collapse of charity in society.[8]

In other words, the foundational perspective brought to bear upon what is happening in life needs to become the experience of God; the human experience of the world must be read from the viewpoint of the Gospel. This starting point necessitates for religious life a repositioning of its energies in formation, pedagogy, and mission. What is required is a move away from speech about community, or the search for new forms that meet popular aspirations, or the lamentation surrounding decline. The phenomena of "event communities" is very real, as is the contemporary experience of the Church as a *societas mixta* and the world as an ambiguous location of good

7 See for examples Evangelii Gaudium, n. 1–8; Laudato Si', n. 1–16, 62–100; Amoris Laetitia, n. 1–30, n. 89–164.

8 A careful reading of the following reflections might prove beneficial in this area: R. A. Markus, "Conversion and Disenchantment in Augustine's Spiritual Career", in: ibid., Sacred and Secular, Studies on Augustine and Latin Christianity, Aldershot/Hampshire/Great Britain 1994, first published 1989); J. Leclercq, La contemplazione di Cristo nel monachesimo medieval, Torino 1994; G. Miccoli, "La proposta cristiana de Francesco d'Assisi", reprinted in Francesco d'Assisi, Realtá e memoria di un'esperienza cristiana, Torino 1991, 33–97; W. Wright, Bond of Perfection: Jeanne de Chantal and Francois de Sales, New York 1985.

and evil. But are religious skilled in addressing not the experience of the transitory event itself or the sinfulness of the Church or the confusing mixture of good and evil in the world, but the God of love and beauty, communion and absolute faithfulness, who is encountered in these circumstances?

The issues confronting vowed religious are not primarily sociological and psychological, nor even those of philosophical truth. Instead, a different public argument is required, a different type of rationality, one less reliant on Aristotle and more dependent on Augustine. On one level, what is needed is a deeper acceptance of the dissolving forces of temporality, the tentativeness of knowledge, and the humility of creatureliness, all of which open up to a distinct image of God as complete Goodness in a post-modern world.[9] The Pontifical Council for Culture reflected on the central theme of the *via pulchritudinis,* viewing this way as a privileged pathway for evangelization in the present society.[10] On another level, in a consumer society driven by market forces and prone to the commodification of all experiences, the challenges of the future will in large measure depend on how the religious-life form itself is able to capture the world of the imagination, the bonding forces of desire and the affections, the will, and the freedom to respond to love by embracing the sacramentality of oneself, the world, the society, and the Church precisely as all of these are signs of a God who is all in all.[11] What is needed is a broadening out of what Pope Benedict referred to as "sacramental mysticism".[12] In language and life there needs to become a focused effort to communicate *a lived experience, symbolization, and intellectualization of the power, faithfulness, beauty of God, and God's operations in history as a God of love. The God of today must become much*

9 See most recently the fine essays in R. Williams, On Augustine, London 2016, especially the chapters on time, the whole Christ, and Christology, 1–24, 25–40, 141–153; C. Harrison, Beauty and Revelation in the Thought of Saint Augustine, Oxford 1992.

10 Pontifical Council for Culture, The Via Pulchritudinis, Privileged Pathway for Evangelisation and Dialogue, Rome 2006; cf. Evangelii Gaudium, n. 167–168.

11 For some recent critical approaches to a consumer society see D. M. Bell Jr., The Economy of Desire: Christianity and Capitalism in a Postmodern World, Grand Rapids/ Michigan 2012; M. T. Eggemeier, A Sacramental-Prophetic Vision, Christian Spirituality in a Suffering World, Collegeville/MN 2014.

12 Benedict XVI, Deus Caritas Est, n. 12–15.

more clearly a God who freely chooses to dwell in bread and who multiplies that bread in the food of daily life.

In the context of a contemporary social fracturing and dissolution of absolutes, there is only one absolute, one common good, capable of embracing the pluralism, disorder, and relativism of current experience: the experience of God, Father, Son and Spirit, as revealed in the economy of God's history with us, most fully expressed in the incarnation, life, crucifixion and death, resurrection, and sending of the Spirit, of the Son. Put slightly differently, religious life is centered neither on community formation, nor on apostolic service, nor on ecclesial witness, nor on an alternative justice-seeking cultural model. All of these are secondary to its core and will take the form needed provided the central experience of the encounter with God is present. What remains to be put in focus is the discovery of an infinite God in the condition of being a finite human.

There are several arresting images in which Pope Francis points to this dimension of religious life. In summary form, I would like to list a few of them in a format parallel to that of Professor Dienberg's:

Thesis 1: The future for religious life in its formation, community, educational, and missionary dimensions lies in its willingness to focus on the mystery of God's encounter with the human experience as revealed in the first covenant and the birth, labors, death, and resurrection of Jesus Christ.

Thesis 2: Institutions previously mediating the experience of God have found themselves compromised, commodified, or relativized, with the result that the world, the Church, and society itself in order to become sacramental and perceived as mediating must be approached from the perspective of the personal experience of God's goodness, faithfulness, and condescension to the human condition. It is no longer the Church that mediates God, but people's faith in God's goodness that allows the Church and the world in their present circumstances to mediate God. Vowed religious witness to this faith.

Thesis 3: In this context (n. 1 & 2), dedicated religious living in a "pluralistic religious landscape" are called to develop a "contemplative gaze", a "horizontal faith" capable of seeing the omni-presence of the Holy Spirit. (*Evangelii Gaudium*, n. 70–71; *Laudato Si'*, n. 96–100; *Amoris Laetitia*, n. 78).

Thesis 4: Communally cultivating this experience of God in the condition of being human, vowed religious live within a "mystical" fraternity "capable of seeing the sacred grandeur of our neighbor, of finding God in every human being, of tolerating the nuisances of life in common by clinging to the love of God, of opening the heart to divine love and seeking the happiness of others just as their heavenly Father does." (*Evangelii Gaudium*, n. 92).

Thesis 5: Committed to the vowed life, religious demonstrate the possibility of "becoming fully human by becoming more than human" by letting "God bring us beyond ourselves in order to attain the fullest truth of our being." (*Evangelii Gaudium*, n. 8) In this light, religious reinterpret their calling to poverty, chastity, and obedience, as a full commitment to complete humanization in the enjoyment and reception of the gift of all things in life and in death; in the affective embrace of every creature; and in the freedom to serve the world in its aspirations for a fulfilment that transcends the world's expectations.

Thesis 6: Conscious of their own epistemological humility and the patient endurance of Jesus Christ, vowed religious are willing to find peace in the mystery of the God of history, the one not able to solve all problems but able instead to bring good out of the not-so-good, the only one who "restores the dead to life and calls into being those things which had not been" (Rom. 4.17; *Deus Caritas Est*, n. 35–36).

* * *

Zusammenfassung zu: Joseph P. Chinnici, Auf der Suche nach einem neuen Wir. Eine Antwort des Evangeliums

Joseph P. Chinnici (Oceanside, CA | USA) geht zunächst auf den soziologischen Befund ein, dass auch in der lebendigen und vielfältigen religiösen Landschaft der USA institutionelle Bindungen schwinden und es außerdem zu einer Kommodifizierung religiöser Erfahrung kommt. Diese Entwicklungen wirken sich natürlich auch auf das Leben religiöser Gemeinschaften und Orden aus.

Chinnici fragt dann, was aus diesen bzw. auf diese Erkenntnisse folgen sollte, da der soziologische Blickwinkel alleine weder ausreichend noch weiterführend ist und außerdem in seiner Massivität beinahe erdrückend auf traditionelles religiöses Leben wirkt. Deswegen schlägt er als alternative und zukünftige Blickwinkel diejenigen vor, die soziologisch nur schwer fassbar sind: Gnade, Glaube und Umkehr. So könnten die Schwierigkeiten von heute zum Wachstumsbeschleuniger des Glaubens von morgen werden.

Um diesen Blickwinkel einnehmen zu können bedarf es aber des religiösen Lebens, womit nicht das Sprechen oder Philosophieren darüber, nicht die Suche nach neuen Formen von Gemeinschaft gemeint ist, sondern eine Erfahrung der Welt vom Evangelium her, eine Fokussierung auf das Wort Gottes.

Verzeichnis der Mitarbeiter*innen // List of Contributors

Joseph P. Chinnici OFM | D. Phil. Oxon.
Präsident und Professor für Geschichte an der Franciscan School of Theology, Oceanside, San Diego CA, USA
// President and Professor of History at Franciscan School of Theology, Oceanside, San Diego CA, USA

Thomas Dienberg OFMCap | Dr. theol., M.A. (Arbeitswissenschaft)
Professor für Theologie der Spiritualität an der Philosophisch-Theologischen Hochschule Münster, Direktor des Kompetenzzentrums für Christliche Spiritualität IUNCTUS Münster
// Professor of Theology of Spirituality / Philosophisch-Theologische Hochschule Münster, Director of IUNCTUS – Competence Centre of Christian Spirituality, Münster

Thomas Eggensperger OP | Dr. theol., M.A. (Philosophie und Spanisch)
Professor für Sozialethik an der Philosophisch-Theologischen Hochschule Münster, Geschäftsführender Direktor des Institut M.-Dominique Chenu Berlin
// Professor of Social Ethics/Philosophisch-Theologische Hochschule Münster, Executive Director of the Institute M.-Dominique Chenu Berlin

Ulrich Engel OP | Dr. theol. habil.
Professor für Philosophisch-theologische Grenzfragen an der Philosophisch-Theologischen Hochschule Münster, Direktor des Institut M.-Dominique Chenu Berlin
// Professor of Philosophical-Theological Crossroads Issues / Philosophisch-Theologische Hochschule Münster, Director of the Institute M.-Dominique Chenu Berlin

Garrett Galvin OFM | PhD (Catholic University of America)
Assistenz-Professor für Bibelwissenschaften und Vizepräsident für Hochschulangelegenheiten an der Franciscan School of Theology, Oceanside, San Diego CA, USA
// Associate Professor of Sacred Scripture and Vice President for Academic Affairs at Franciscan School of Theology, Oceanside, San Diego CA, USA

Mareike Gerundt | Dipl.-Theol., M.A. (Organisationsmanagement und Spiritualität)
Wissenschaftliche Mitarbeiterin im Kompetenzzentrum für Christliche Spiritualität IUNCTUS Münster
// Resident Fellow at IUNCTUS – Competence Centre for Christian Spirituality, Münster

Bernd Janzen | Dr. theol., Ph.D, San Diego/CA

Manuela Kalsky | Dr. theol.
Professorin und Inhaberin des Edward Schillebeeckx-Lehrstuhls für Theologie und Gesellschaft, Vrije Universiteit Amsterdam, Direktorin des Dominicaans Studiecentrum voor Theologie en Samenleving
// Professor and Chair Holder of the Edward Schillebeeckx-Chair for Theology and Society / Vrije Universiteit Amsterdam, Director of the Dominicaans Studiecentrum voor Theologie en Samenleving

Karl Heinz Knubel | Unternehmer, Münster
Entrepreneur, Münster

Bernhard Kohl OP | Dr. des. theol.
Wissenschaftlicher Mitarbeiter am Institut M.-Dominique Chenu Berlin, Visiting Scholar 2017 am Dominican Institute of Toronto, Canada
// Resident Fellow at the Institute M.-Dominique Chenu Berlin, Visiting Scholar 2017 at the Dominican Institute of Toronto, Canada

José de Jesús Legorreta Zapeda | Dr. rer. soc., Dr. theol.
Professor für Religionssoziologie an der Universidad Iberoamericana, México Ciudad – Santa Fé, México
// Professor of Sociology of Religión / Universidad Iberoamericana, México Ciudad – Santa Fé, México

Franziska Madl OP | MMag. theol.
Novizenmeisterin der Dominikanerinnen in Wien-Hacking
// Novice Master of the Dominican Sisters in Vienna-Hacking

Ángel F. Méndez Montoya OP | Dr. theol., Lic. phil., Lic. en Danza
Vollzeit-Professor im Department Religionswissenschaft an der Universidad Iberoamericana, México Ciudad – Santa Fé, México; Non Resident Fellow am Institut M.-Dominique Chenu Berlin
// Professor at the Department of Religious Studies / Universidad Iberoamericana, México Ciudad – Santa Fé, México; Non Resident Fellow at the Institut M.-Dominique Chenu Berlin

Sharon Padilla | BA (Lit.), MA (Theol.), MA (Ecumenical Studies)
Übersetzerin, Doktorandin (Neues Testament) an der Universität Bonn
// Interpreter, Post-Graduate Student (New Testament), University of Bonn

Michaela Pfadenhauer | Dr. phil.
Professorin für Soziologie am Institut für Soziologie der Universität Wien
// Professor for Sociology at the Institute for Sociology / University of Vienna

Monseñor Raúl Vera López OP | Ing., Lic. theol.
Bischof von Saltillo, Mexiko
// Bishop of Saltillo, Mexico

Stephan Winter | Dr. theol. habil., M.A. (phil.)
Professor für Liturgiewissenschaft an der Philosophisch-Theologischen Hochschule Münster, Leiter des Fachbereichs „Zeitdiagnostik" am Kompetenzzentrum für Christliche Spiritualität IUNCTUS Münster
// Professor of Liturgics / Philosophisch-Theologische Hochschule Münster, Head of the department "Zeitdiagnostik", IUNCTUS – Competence Centre for Christian Spirituality, Münster